EXPLORING THOMAS AQUINAS
ESSAYS and SERMONS

M.-D. Chenu, O.P.
Yves Congar, O.P.
Jean-Pierre Torrell, O.P.
C.J. Pinto de Oliveira, O.P.
Walter Principe, C.S.B.
Edward Schillebeeckx, O.P.
Karl Rahner, S.J.

Translations by
Thomas F. O'Meara, O.P.

NEW PRIORY PRESS
EXPLORING THE DOMINICAN MISSION

EXPORING THOMAS AQUINAS

Copyright © 2017 by the Dominican Province of St. Albert the Great (U.S.A.) All rights reserved.

Published by New Priory Press
1910 South Ashland Avenue
Chicago, IL 60608-2903
NewPrioryPress.com

Table of Contents

Original Sources vi

Introduction vii

ESSAYS

M.-D. Chenu, O.P., "Thomas Aquinas, an Innovator in a New World" 1

Yves Congar, O.P., "The Historicity of the Human Person according to Thomas Aquinas" 19
- I 19
- II 22
- III 23
- IV 26
- V 28

Jean-Pierre Torrell, O.P., "Saracens and Thomas Aquinas" 31

Yves Congar, O.P., "The Theology of the Church in Thomas Aquinas" 41

C.J. Pinto de Oliveira, O.P. "Thomas Aquinas, Vatican II, and Contemporary Theology" 55
- I. The Vicissitudes of Thomism and the Presence of Thomas Aquinas and the Directions of the Second Vatican Council 56
  - A. Thomism before the Council and Thomas Aquinas' Thought at the Council 56
  - B. The Doctrine of Aquinas and the Basic Directions of the Council 60

      C. Thomas Aquinas: The Commendation of the Council 64
- II. Questions and Issues Coming from Major Currents of Contemporary Theology 67
  - A. Positive or Critical Assumptions.......... 67
  - B. A Triple Challenge: Theologies of Existence, History, and Liberation 68
- III. Recent Theological Directions and Thomas Aquinas 72
  - A. Thomas Aquinas and the Crisis of Foundational Theology 73
  - B. A True Fundamental Theology 75

Walter Principe, C.S.B., "Aquinas' Spirituality for Christ's Faithful Living in the World" 83

Some Historical Background 84
Early Church Theologians 87
Other Historical Forces at Work 89
Some Particular Themes in Thomas Aquinas 95
    (a) Giving value to the uniqueness of each person's spirituality 95
    (b) An ecological principle 96
    (c) The wholeness of the human person: passions or emotions as sharing morality. 96
    (d) The human person as image of God and of the Trinity 98
      (e) Finding the will of God 100
      (f) A spirituality of prudence guided by the Holy Spirit 101
      (g) The New Law and the gifts of the Holy Spirit 102
      (h) Faith in God in contrast with propositions of faith and ecclesial teaching 103
      (i) The presence of Christ to human history 105

SERMONS

M.-D. Chenu, O.P., "Veritas Liberabit Vos. 'The Truth Will Make You Free'" 109
    Veritas Liberabit Vos. "The Truth Will Make You Free" 109
    The Spiritual Liberty of Thomas Aquinas 110
    Aquinas' Contact with his Contemporaries 112
    Our Spiritual Freedom 114

Edward Schillebeeckx, O.P., "Thomas Aquinas, Servant of the Word" 117

Karl Rahner, S.J., "Thomas Aquinas: Friar, Theologian, and Mystic" 123
    Thomas the Monk 124
    Thomas the Theologian 125
    Thomas The Mystic 127

Selected Writings on Thomas Aquinas' Theology 129

SIX ESSAYS: ORIGINAL SOURCES

M.-D. Chenu, O.P., "S. Thomas, Innovateur dans la créativité d'un monde nouveau," *Tommaso d'Aquino nella Storia del Pensiero I. Le Fonti del Pensiero di S. Tommaso* (Naples: Edizioni Domenicane Italiane, 1974) 39-50

Yves Congar, O.P., "L'Historicité de l'homme selon Thomas d'Aquin," *Doctor Communis* 22 (1969): 293-304

Jean-Pierre Torrell, O.P., "Saint Thomas et les non-chrétiens," *Revue Thomiste* 106 (2006): 35-49

Yves Congar, O.P., *Église de Saint Augustin à l'époque moderne* (Paris: Cerf, 1970) 232-40

C. J. Pinto de Oliveira, O.P., "Saint Thomas, le concile et la théologie contemporaine" *Nova et Vetera* 56 (1981): 161 185

Walter Principe, C.S.B., "Aquinas' Sprituality for Christ's Faithful Living in the World," *Spirituality Today* 44 (1992): 110-131

THREE SERMONS: ORIGINAL SOURCES

Marie-Dominique Chenu, O.P., "*Veritate Liberabit Vos. La Vérité vous rendra libres*" (Jn. 8, 32), *Sources* 16 (1990): 97-106

Edward Schillebeexkx, O.P., "Thomas Aquinas: Servant of the Word," Robert Schreiter, ed., The Schillebeeckx Reader (New Yourk: Crossroad, 1984) 288-291; the original source is "Kritisch geloofsdenken als eredienst en apostolaat," *Neerlandia Dominicana* 20 (1965): 77-80

Karl Rahner, S.J., "Thomas Aquinas: Friar, Theologian and Mystc," *Cross and Crown* 20 (1968) 5-9; a translation of "Thomas von Aquin als Mönch, Theologe, Mystiker," *Korrespondenzblatt des Priestergebetsvereines im Canisianum zu Innsbruck* 86 (1952): 89-93

Introduction
Thomas F. O'Meara, O.P.

Thomas Aquinas—he has influenced an extraordinary number of men and women. The recent 800th Anniversary of the founding of the Dominican Order bears witness to how his thought has reached through centuries thousands of teachers, writers, and preachers from Croatia to the Philippines, from Peru to Armenia.

Aquinas' theology led Catherine of Siena to urge reform on the papacy, and it inspired the Renaissance painter, Fra Angelico. The Dominican Archbishop, Diego de Deza, advised Christopher Columbus to explore what lay to the west of Portugal, while a little later Bartolomé de Las Casas defended the rights of the Native Americans against the Spanish conquerors. In this century, his principles of intellectual life influenced M. J. Lagrange to begin a modern school of Catholic biblical studies in Jerusalem, and guided Yves Congar to pioneer a Roman Catholic acceptance of ecumenism. Novelists as different as Sigrid Undset and Flannery O'Connor have learned from the pages of Aquinas. Bishops have condemned him and popes have praised him.

The Twentieth Century rediscovered Thomas Aquinas. The seven scholars contributing to this book continue the work of Martin Grabmann, A.D. Sertillanges, Norberto del Prado, Reginald Garrigou-Lagrange, Étienne Gilson, and Bernard Lonergan. The attention given to Aquinas after 1900 in historical research and intellectual forms led to Vatican II where his thought addressed modernity and stimulated pastoral renewal. Aquinas' theology in the course of the Twentieth Century came to exist in several modes: (1) a philosophical and limited neo-Thomism; (2) historical research on medieval thinkers; (3) applications of Thomism to ethical and political issues; (4) dialogues between Aquinas and modern philosophers; and (5) expansive studies of grace present in the church's life and human history. Furthermore, the Twentieth Century produced an expansion of Aquinas' thinking, one active in psychology and aesthetics, in the forms of human journey and cultural history, in being and grace, and in the church beyond law and penetrated by ministerial grace.

The following articles present seven interpreters of Aquinas in the Twentieth Century who are transmitting and applying his insights.

ESSAYS

Thomas Aquinas, an Innovator in a New World
M.-D. Chenu, O.P.

"Having been named a bachelor-professor and beginning to unveil what his quiet personality had held in his spirit, Friar Thomas appeared to have received from God remarkable knowledge. He surpassed all the professors. In his courses he stated new problems, discovered new methods, and used new sequences of proofs. To hear him teach was to be in contact with a new doctrine supported by new argumentation. One could not doubt that God by touching him with a new light and with a newness of inspiration led him to teach, from the beginning of his professorship, openly and directly, in word and in writing, new views."[1] These are the words of William of Tocco, the most extensive biographer of Thomas Aquinas. He was qualified to describe this because he had heard Aquinas lecture at the University of Naples from 1272 to 1274. Later he was one of those who convinced Pope John XXII to begin the process of canonization. One can hardly avoid noting that, in these ten lines, the word "*novus*" appears eight times. This must be an intentional repetition. Is not the word itself a direct indication of the situation William observed?

I am emphasizing the frequency of the word "new" because the documents of the Church in the past century treating Aquinas never mention this aspect. In fact, those Church documents envision mainly a "*philosophia perennis*," something outside of time and space, a teaching valuable in itself but beyond any instance of newness and change.

---

[1] William of Tocco, *Ystoria sancti Thomae de Aquino* (Toronto: Pontifical Institute of Medieval Studies, 1996) ch. 15, 121-122.

In William's view, Friar Thomas, stimulated by the cultural changes of his time, found them an impetus to give newness to teaching. Content and method, spirit and technique, principles and conclusion, style and inspiration – all the elements of this lofty knowledge of God came together to manifest a new kind of theology. The encounter of faith with a new culture was the reason and the motivation for this theology. Here we have an eminent case and a daring lesson in the difficult encounter that takes place whenever culture moves in a significant way towards the new.

Novus, novitas. Looking at Aquinas' use of words with "new" in their root is informative. Today we see the pride which the new brings to the course of social evolution, to the various sectors of science and culture, to the categories of scholars or the media, and to institutions. They all offer an important context for the enterprise of Thomas Aquinas within the coherent phenomena of civilization.

"New" is the appropriate adjective expressly given to Gothic architecture in full creative expansion after the Romanesque period. That extraordinary flourishing of cathedrals includes a church which Friar Thomas walked past in his daily life: Notre Dame in Paris. A strengthening of verticality and at the same time the horizontal strength of the ogival supports and the vaults permit the walls to sustain considerable weight and to open more and more space for windows of light. The splendor of the cathedral's beauty is the effect of a rigorous calculation of forces not possible up to that time. It is not just a romantic cliché that there are parallels between the cathedrals of stone and the *summae* of theology. They are a dual domain of cultural creation. Rational enterprises in different disciplines can be legitimately interpreted by each other: they express both rationality and mystery. There is a homology of phenomena in medieval civilization.

A new style of decoration in sculpture represented in a naturalistic way things, plants, and animals. We see human persons in their daily activities, their jobs; we see their expressions and their personalities. This style replaced an imagination of fantasy, an empty corporeality, and the symbolic monsters of Romanesque sculpture. Now all of humanity located—in the Christian mystery where Christ is the brother of men and women—appeared in an earthly imagery with real surroundings. The world passed from allegory to natural science.

In the world of literature, poets and theoreticians had a vital awareness (sometimes aggressively stated against the opponents of this modernity) of new directions in speculative grammar, literary analysis, and technical categories. Matthew of Vendôme, fifty years before Aquinas, proclaimed in his *Ars poetica*: "In our time what is arriving has put to an end the old."[2] The novel replaced the narrative song; the refined poetry of courtly life replaced the descriptions of wars in the feudal era. In new forms and values a purification of sensibility and a refinement of emotions occurred. To give a classical analysis of this modernism of new generations, Ovid was rediscovered. A small work that was particularly read and re-read is *De Amore* where André le Chapelain puts into scholastic form in 1184 the doctrine of courtly love.[3] That book will be condemned in 1277 at the same time that Thomas Aquinas was being condemned as a naturalist. Dante will soon appear as the central witness to this new art, while Brunetto

---

[2] Matthew of Vendôme, *Ars versificatoria*, Edmond Faral, ed., *Les Arts poétiques du XIIe et du XIIIe siècle* (Paris, 1924) 109-123.

[3] Andreas Capellanus, *De amore et amoris remedio*, P.G. Walsh, ed. (New York, 1983).

Latini, a contemporary of Aquinas and Secretary of the Communità of Florence, has composed in French an allegorical poem on nature and love under the title *The Book of the Treasure*, an encyclopedia of the history of the world and the laws of society.[4] Dante, who did not like him, will say that he taught "how man can be eternal."[5]

Whatever ambiguity there might be in an ethics of the world of courtly sensibility, still it bears witness to the dawn of a positive awareness of the perceptions and values of interior experience. Abelard (who was also a knight of the new logic against a vulgarly objective casuistry) authored poems in the courtly style for his Eloise. He reintroduced the primacy of the intention in the evaluation of human actions even as he reduced the role of the minister in the sacrament of penance. Opposing his bishop in Paris, William of Auvergne, Thomas Aquinas will support the subjective criterion of conscience. This discovery of the subject does not at all block the dialectical analysis of the age considering objects. The new sciences reveal their structures, causes, and rules. They bring a depth not only to the epistemology of knowing but also to the description of the human person.

The study of ancient writings is being rediscovered: it vitalized a variety of disciplines and reestablished the philosophy of Aristotle, discovered little by little in successive waves of translations (from Arabic and Greek). Aristotle draws the curiosity of the age to physics and politics. Psychology and ethics are now understood in a higher way as human sciences. Empiricism opposes ideology.

---

[4] Brunetto Latini, *The Book of the Treasure*, Paul Barrette and Spurgeon Baldwin, eds. (New York, 1993).
[5] Dante, *The Divine Comedy*, *Inferno*, XV.

AN INNOVATOR IN A NEW WORLD

Should we call that age imitative? No, it is a renaissance, a new birth. The intoxication it aroused in so many led the conservatives to stand against the *novatores* of the University of Paris (as later they stood against the Renaissance in Florence). That era inspired those seeking something new to follow models. Aquinas does not imitate Aristotle any more than the Gothic artists imitate the art of antiquity, or the poets of courtly love imitate the *ars amandi* of Ovid. In all this Dante is an outstanding witness of true creativity.

One knows that Albert the Great, the teacher of Friar Thomas, had to the amazement of many and despite official prohibitions sought "to render Aristotle intelligible to the Latins."[6] This enterprise produced tremors lasting fifty years; the results were striking in higher studies, sacred as well as profane, where Aquinas developed his world-view. At that time, new generations sought realism; realism takes a special form in the raw naturalism of the *Roman de la Rose* of Jean de Meung who lived near Friar Thomas on the Rue Saint-Jacques. One cannot read Thomas without pondering this cultural relationship with Jean de Meung as well as with Dante in the following generation. Is Dante a disciple of St. Thomas? This is a good question, for at first Dante and Thomas seem to be likeminded witnesses to the same mentality.

Institutions too, both those of the church and of the state, were being drawn into these changes, even as they provoked them. In secular society, there were new forms of economic and political life, emerging sometimes with violence. Little by little the feudal regime lost its reason to exist and much of its efficacy. Guilds and communes set up bonds of solidarity among people outside the paternalistic authority of the lords. A

---

[6] Albert the Great, *Physica* 1, tract. 1, ch. 1.

social field of new experiences, unforeseen structures, and a wider political consciousness seemed to represent a regime of God. Those "cultural communes" called universities were founded in an independence from the monastic schools who in the new kind of cities were increasingly marginalized. The universities are the places for learning, cultural and spiritual. Friar Thomas cannot be conceived outside of them; they are his environment. If he had stayed at Monte Cassino according to the feudal hope of his parents, he would not have been Thomas Aquinas. Similarly, Francis of Assisi cannot be imagined outside the world of people with their trades or outside of the new social connections social of the world of business and production in which he recreates the evangelical power of the word "brothers." Thomas and Francis, out of social change and out of the Gospel message, challenge the church's feudalism.

Patterns of change, an atmosphere of change, contagious alterations moving from institution to institution and from individual to individual influence the enterprise of Aquinas as he was conceiving his works and writing them down. This is his world: this is the society in which he reads the Bible in a new way and in which he looks in a new way at the intellectual life of antiquity. To understand faith, a new theology emerges, one aspiring to be a wisdom but faithfully fashioned by the mystery of an incomprehensible God.

That age, far from reducing the value of theology, gave it a deeper expression through the truth of incarnation. The theology of Aquinas has value certainly in its conclusions but even more in its systematic construction. This importance comes in a basic way from the lucid and direct encounter with the culture of his time. It was a time when faith and structure in the church were also being flooded by the ideas of ancient culture. Thanks to the translations of great works of antiquity, scientific and not only philosophical texts, the metaphysical principles of Aristotle and Plato presented in professorial elaborations led to a keen intellectual awareness of the dignity of *nature* and the demands of *reason*. The resurgence of nature, reason, human realities provoked in the young universities of the West (Paris, Bologna, Naples, Oxford, Cologne) a strong reaction against feudal conservatism, passive faith, and a monastic church.

The result was unique and complex and (as in our own times) dramatic. Without doubt the key point is the conception of the human person. Anthropology calls forth, even determines theology (as it does today). When God speaks to people, he speaks the language of people.

The orientation of Aquinas (underlying his many writings) goes contrary to the dualism inherited from Augustine according to which the soul exists apart from the body in a mainly spiritual zone. Does the soul inhabit the body like a boat or prison? Aquinas says, No. There is a consubstantial unity for matter and spirit; a reciprocal coexistence and a common activity. Everything emerges in matter and everything is penetrated by spirit. In a unique form, not only do I have a body but I am my body. All that is in my intellect comes from outside, from what is coming through my senses. There is no totally autonomous interiority. If here the immortality of the soul is questioned and death seems to be an absurdity, still the beatific vision gives the presence of the body an element of a perfect happiness. On earth emotions are physiological and corporeal realities, places for virtues and not just as little pockets of spiritual activity.

The human person is entirely one with the cosmos. Human nature lives in nature; it is a microcosm of nature. The material world is not just a backdrop against which the history of peoples in their cultures as well as in their salvation and damnation is played out. The history of nature is not just a minor event in the theater of a spiritual history. If this were true, the human person would be a stranger whose true country is beyond this world and its history in a kingdom of pure spirit and divine ideas. The history of nature would unfold with necessity, and the journey of being a human would move forward without any pauses or difficulties.

With a quite different perspective, Aquinas observed the inclusion of the history of nature in the history of spirit. The history of spirit is the history of nature. The human person is situated at the juncture of those two worlds which even with their essential distinctions realize in the human being a homogeneity of spirit and matter.

The reaction to the new thinking was violent: not only among the professors who taught theology but among all those in the society who were interested in what was spiritual. Aquinas was strongly attacked, and the attack has lasted through the centuries.

Since a person is a person precisely in a unity of matter and spirit, the human being finds fulfillment, its happiness, in the fashioning the world amid human solidarity with others. Social by nature and yet individual by matter, people are drawn together. The existence of the universe does not take place in fragile movements endangering human interior life but in the economy and interplay of all of creation. The entire field of culture groans with the sorrow of giving birth as it longs for the revelation of the offspring of God, a process reaching to new heavens and new earths. In this way, the plan of the creator gives to the destiny of the human person a role and function belonging to matter.

Is this Aristotle's thought? Yes. In his instrument of analysis—experimental method and a rigorous formulation of the "unity of forms"—this is Aristotelian. Still, at the level of a more radical inspiration, this is also the meaning of the Incarnation. Thus, a hidden motivation is evangelical.

The basis of this anthropological option—the discovery of nature in its consistency and even dignity—brought controversies. Thomas avoids the temptation to sacralize. He does not need to refer the forces of nature to God in a way that absorbs them; he does not need to refer nature to ideas or place it in an infantile conception of providence prone to the miraculous. Previously imagination basically formed a mirage of a distant supernatural world projected on to things and people. We see that approach in Romanesque art and in that age's social customs and laws. Now, in different ways nature discovers its profane reality even as it assumes a religious value, one coming from God. Nature is not just a mirror. Nature *is*; things *are*. They are solid, structured, sensual, intimate. They are *good* not simply as derived from the goodness of God but in themselves. The world has a profane dimension, and to recognize that in nature is truly to give glory to God. Albert the Great declared (not without some aggressiveness): "When I study nature, I do not expect to come upon miracles."[7]

Paradoxically one can find support for Albert the natural scientist in Francis of Assisi's *Canticle of Canticles* where the glory of God is found in the discovery of nature. This vision is quite different from that of monasticism: it expresses and confirms the "brotherhood" of the human person with living realities,

---

[7] Albert the Great, *De generatione et corruptione* I, 1.22.

with my "brother" the sun, my "sister" the moon, with the wind, water, and death.

The new academic disciplines meet in the life of the universities. The *Timaeus* of Plato and the *Physics* of Aristotle are influential not only in the schools but in the mentality of Jean de Meung; that mentality is evident in Ovid as well as in Roman law (which is undergoing its own renaissance). The Roman system of law aims at organizing the world and the state (St. Louis IX and the Emperor Frederick) by passing beyond an outmoded paternalism. There is a search for a responsible theory of how power exists in rational procedures of justice; there is an observation that judgments attributed to God have too often been grounded in false mysticism. Parallel discoveries in nature and in society, however, proceed, as often happens, along with theories of providence in God and gratuitous grace in Christian economy (theories that might seem to be threatening and seducing human liberty). This is a time of "secularization" with its ambiguities. And, in the Thirteenth Century, in an Augustinian atmosphere, all this is a scandal. The condemnation of 1277, an understandable reaction of Christendom, confronts this scandal in a deformed way.

In his theology of creation bringing together the divine government and the economy of grace, Aquinas emphasized Christian values as he followed the line of St. Augustine. Moving in another direction, however, he introduced a full autonomy for nature and liberty. God who has constituted nature does not hold back from natural beings precisely what is proper to their natures.[8] If this is a metaphysical axiom, it is also a mystical principle. Indeed, it is the key to the spirituality of Thomas Aquinas. Bonaventure, his Franciscan colleague

---

[8] See Aquinas, *Summa theologiae* I, 45, 5 and 7.

at the University of Paris, in fraternal opposition day after day, will be a voice for the Augustinian view. For him the truth of things is their truth in the eternal thought of God. The full existence of things is found only in God; their descent into time brings their fragility. Fulfilled understanding cannot be acquired through science alone but only through divine illumination.

After nature, reason. If reason is nature, still reason has a special place because it gives the understanding of nature, of *physis* and *logos*. The word itself, "*ratio*," in the language of the time denominates "essence" and "concept." Reason has the power of discovery, of discerning how to measure the causes of things not solely by referring them to the Supreme Cause but in their inner reality. Certainly, an underlying movement carries the person through instinct and implicit desire towards God as do the essence and reality of the beings of nature discovered through the method of Aristotle's *Analytica*. But then, how to avoid a shock when faith comes face to face with the rationality of science? How to commune with mystery in the obscurity of a faith where reason cannot know all the causalities in the divine will?

The encounter of faith with nature is two-sided. First, there is the autonomy of profane sciences with their own laws and specific objects, their own irreducible epistemological fields. The sciences in all areas are valid in themselves and for themselves. There is a general law: no scholar can recognize, demonstrate, or reject a proposition except in virtue of its principles, that is, out the core of that science. This categorical axiom is proclaimed by the strict Aristotelians who were disciples at the faculty of liberal arts of the Arab philosopher Averroes. Among them were Boethius of Denmark (a worthy partner of Thomas in methodological clarity and a humanist of a high level) and the more famous Siger of Brabant, head of the movement and an agitator. People composing lists of heretics place him in hell, but Dante in his *Paradiso* puts him in the fourth heaven, that of light.[9] Thomas argued with those teachers but continued to hold their interest and friendship, and they waited impatiently for his new works. In fact, Thomas responded to their request to reconsider the meaning of the cliché among the theologians that the profane sciences are only servants, *ancillae*, of theology. Yes, he said, they serve, but in the measure that they are themselves.

The refusal of any intellectual theocracy was not without risk and danger. A serious challenge came when reason (permitted to be itself with its curiosity, its organic diversity, and its criteria) seeks to introduce itself into faith. Theology is literally an understanding of faith, a *logos* of the human person assumed by the *Logos* of God. If the Word of God is proclaimed in human concepts, the logic of this humanization might imply that human intelligence lacks reverence for transcendent mystery. Do not too many questions bring an alienation in the darkness of faith? Nonetheless, Thomas said, reason offers its resources to an active, conscious, organic, and critical elaboration of faith; that process reaches the point of constituting theology which is a "science" in an Aristotelian sense of the word. This aroused the resistance of his contemporaries (in fact, only Thomas held this position): in this terrain of profane terms and categories mystics shy away, and simple believers are shocked. After 1231, in the charter founding the University of Paris, Gregory IX had warned the theologians against using pagan terminologies. Precisely at that moment Friar Bonaventure during his lecture at the University reproached Aquinas in a

---

[9] Dante, *The Divine Comedy*, Paradiso, X.

friendly way by saying that he turned the pure wine of the Word of God into water. Eight days later, in his own classroom Thomas answered: it is just as it was at Cana where water is transformed into good wine. What let him recognize reason's power was a fearless evangelical grace. This occurred in a cultural context, a milieu of ideas, writings, and artistic creations. It was "an age of reason."[10] Thomas is the teacher - better, the prophet - of this age, the era of the gothic cathedrals with marvels of architectonic reason and of *summae* in theology constructed out of questions and reasons.

Aquinas did meet opposition. A continuing conflict, often violent, overshadowed the importance of the Angelic Doctor. Those controversies are highlighted by documents from different episodes written by those taking part in them. Let us recall a tempestuous evening assembly with a prominent disputation in the presence of the bishop of Paris. That disputation *de quodlibet* was held at the end of the turbulent year 1270.[11] We have two texts of the academic event: one comes from the main adversary of Thomas, John Peckham, regent of the rival school, reactionary Augustinian, and "*homo pomposus*" as one chronicle calls him. The other text is placed by the Dominican friars in the collection *Vitae fratrum*. The two documents give different interpretations, but both describe the context and climate of the conflict. For his *quodlibet* disputations we have a rapid redaction by Thomas himself, a presentation developed amid the quarrels. The topics are the human person as body and soul, the unity of the intellect, individuation through matter, the eternity of the world, the relationship of the world to God, and others. Some of the masters in arts debated these issues

---

[10] See Georges Duby, *Foundations of a New Humanism* (Cleveland, 1968).
[11] Quodlibet XII of the critical year 1270 holds twenty-four disputations.

too, and so Thomas finds himself between two fronts; the truth of Aristotle (but with his views compromised by Averroes), and theological tradition represented by Augustinianism.

In December, 1270, the corporation of the masters in theology at Paris, the highest doctrinal body of judgment in the church at that time, condemns thirteen propositions presenting theories of Averroist Aristotelianism taught by certain masters. Indirectly this compromised Thomas Aquinas, for he may have seen his positions included in the two propositions added at the last moment. Nonetheless, this intervention of authority did not calm down the debate that dealt with the autonomous value of philosophy.

Aquinas left Paris in 1272 and following his superiors' request went to the University of Naples. The controversy remained very active in Paris. Bonaventure in his university lectures continued to denounce any separate philosophy. In 1277, three years after the death of the Dominican, the theologians of Paris under the presidency of the bishop promulgated a syllabus of 219 propositions. It was a summary list (disordered, provocative, shrewd) against what was seen as rationalism and naturalism entering into the milieu of the University. In this movement there was an erotic naturalism (as in the work of André le Chapelain) and even a criticism of the Bible as a collection of myths. There is too a cosmic determinism freezing human liberty and a denial of the resurrection. The bishop's text speaks of the many errors "both in the arts as well as in theology" and rejected the entire epistemological approach of the time. A dozen propositions touched expressly Aquinas and his disciples.

Some have said that the condemnation of 1277 decided the evolution of Western thought up to the beginnings of modern times. Under a universal competence of philosophical reason the profane sciences remain autonomous outside the positions of faith. Repercussions continued and expanded; eleven years later the Archbishop of Canterbury (with some agreement from the University of Oxford), Robert Kilwardby (a Dominican like Aquinas), issued similar decisions, particularly in anthropology. In 1281 and then again in 1286, both times at Oxford, the old adversary John Peckham - he had become Archbishop of Canterbury - renewed the condemnation against a certain *novella quaedam philosophia* opposing the teaching of Augustine. The words "new philosophy" recall our opening citation from William of Tocco; at Oxford, however, it was used with derision.

To those violent doctrinal controversies was added institutional interference. In arguments over the positions of Aquinas the hostility of the professors of the university to the mendicant orders played a large role. Was not the very originality of the mendicants fragmenting tradition? Were not the friars ruining the monastic form of religious life and the ministerial structures of the church? Two times during the second period when Aquinas taught in Paris (from 1252 to 1260 with William of Saint-Amour and from 1268 to 1272 with Gérard of Abbeville) the Friars Preachers and the Friars Minor were threatened. The problem returns often in the topics of the professors' *quodlibet* disputations. It interests us here because that reactionary conservatism denounced "the new Apostles" as false prophets and as precursors of the Antichrist.

In that unhappy atmosphere of quarrels the opponents were not lacking in perception, and the authorities were not insensitive to the issues. What they denounced, without seeing its authentic dynamism, was the rebirth of the Gospel realized by the mendicants.

who examined critically the purpose of the structures and hierarchies of the church which had been in place for centuries. The friars' fraternity with its particular poverty, a witness to the Spirit, seemed to be nourished by the myth of a return to the primitive church. A dwelling on the past can be subversive. It is not a question then of a conflict between secular clergy and members of religious orders over benefices. The basic problem touches the existence of a new kind of Christian life where a prophetic message might criticize economic, political, and clerical structures and might counter the ideologies supporting them. William of Saint-Amour and his colleagues would not accept any change in the church. They did not admit the church's power to have new forms and did not accept the realization of the Gospel in new ways under the presence of the Spirit.

Change always arrives with ambiguity. Ambiguity brought real risks like the groups of "Spirituals" in the mendicant orders. Their extravagant and antisocial strictness—they indirectly supported the critique of those clinging to the past—threatened the equilibrium of institutions and of doctrines. Eventually they fell into disgrace before the Roman Church. Regardless, the changes in the world and society, and the understanding of the human person provoked fresh readings of the Gospel and gave opportunities for the church to liberate itself from dead theological and ecclesiastical structures.

Being set free and living amid new possibilities, developing a perspective for a new spiritual geography, and pursuing a religious dynamic helped some to survive that double crisis, doctrinal and institutional. In encounters with new cultures, there were new directions in social organizations and law. Beyond its basis in tradition, law seized a happy occasion to find a new creative energy to implant itself in new human areas (including the Incarnation) and to assist the church in being planted in the world. Theology ceased to be an ideology of an established regime; going beyond a short-sighted empiricism, it offers a prophetic viewpoint as basic. Theology found a personal and scientific methodology—and too an objective elaboration in the community. This was not a frivolous concession to the fashion of the moment; rather, the very message of faith gave birth to a theology which is psychologically and theologically healthy. Grace leads nature to comprehend itself in a cultural density and historicity.

Cultural dimensions in the course of history go beyond academic teaching. They emerge in new images and lead the religious dimension to find new mental categories and vocabularies. There are new disciplines like sciences treating the human person. At that moment the encrusted framework of the seven liberal arts (taught out of an exhausted pedagogy as the successor to the Roman world and feudal humanism) opened up. Albert the Great, Thomas' teacher, wrote that science was far from complete. New sciences await discovery. It is quite significant that Thomas' approach included intellectual friendships with the professors of the liberal arts in Paris who sought after his death to be given the body of their former colleague. Theology appeared as a historical dimension of the life of the church at the same time as the life of the church enters into the breadth of theology.

Thomas Aquinas' enterprise found a certain check. His canonization in 1323 did not erase fully the effect of the condemnation of 1277. Posthumous glory did not support the anthropology of Aquinas or his epistemological clarity. Later the Christian fabric was covered over by a Jansenist Augustinianism and a Cartesian dualism.

Did not Vatican II bring a correction in the concept of the human person and in the philosophy of nature and the autonomy of reason? Precisely because the church is vitally conscious of change in the world and of a new era just begun, the celebration of the seventh centenary of Aquinas' birth gives voice to this hope in the difficult meeting of theology and new cultures. Aquinas is not only an official doctor but the representative of an evangelical movement which made the Word of God contemporary—and this is how he appears in the witness of William of Tocco.

We conclude with some poetry, a few lines from a woman, a Beguine of Anvers, Hedwig, almost a contemporary of Thomas Aquinas, who also sang of newness, of newness as the challenge and gift of love and of grace.[12]

> Love is ever new.
> And she revives every day!
> Those who renew themselves she causes to be born again
> To continual acts of goodness.
> How can anyone
> Remain old, fainthearted at Love's presence?
> Such a person lives truly old in sadness,
> Always with little profit;
> For he has lost sight of the new path,
> And he is denied the newness
> That lies in new service of Love,
> In the nature of the love of new lovers.

---

[12] Hadewijch d'Anvers. *Poemes de Beguines* (Paris, 1954) 62; in English, *Hadewijch*, "Poems in Stanzas": *The Complete Works* (Mahwah, 1980) 145.

The Historicity of the Human Person According to Thomas Aquinas
Yves Congar, O.P.

It is risky, even dangerous, to ask a thinker to give an answer to a question he never asked. Nonetheless, it is legitimate to read an author not only in light of what preceded him, his sources, but also in light of what has come after him. We can look for his thinking to be seminal: we can uncover seeds which in this theology did not find a full fruition, although they enabled what follows. This is simply to recognize more fully the richness and the limitations of that thinking. We appreciate it from the perspective of themes that are seen more clearly today. In this spirit we want to ask Thomas Aquinas about an aspect of human nature: the historicity of the human person.

This topic is very much the concern of modern philosophers. Not a few have reproached Aquinas with lacking a sense of history. Did he not substitute a Greek (Stoic or Aristotelian) view for the concrete and historical one of the Bible? Obviously Aquinas does not offer the view of historicity found in modern phenomenology. And too, the medieval Dominican does present human nature as rather circumscribed and less self-aware. Still, without exhausting this topic, we want to show that there is a true historicity in his theology.

I

An attentive study of a cluster of important theological themes and conclusions shows that Aquinas sought a way of thinking that occupied itself less and less with participation in exemplary causality and more and more with final causes. There is a dynamic in the actions through which a human person matures and freely opens up the self towards the goal of life. M.-J. Le Guillou has shown how charity, the form of the virtues, is treated in the *Summa theologiae* as a "movement of the rational creature towards God." Love is a dynamic; it forms the *activities* of virtues, drawing them together as they move toward their destiny. A similar approach is found in other areas of Aquinas' theology. For instance, in developing a theology of the Holy Spirit dwelling in the soul, the *Commentary on the Sentences* stresses conformity to the divine exemplar, while later the *Summa theologiae* emphasizes the acts by which the soul can touch God as an object of knowledge and of love. A second example is the way in which the *Summa theologiae* presents the gifts of the Holy Spirit from the point of view of movement towards the goal.[1] That movement is properly divine as it passes beyond the efforts and limits of the virtuous human conscience (*ST* I-II, 48, 1 and 3).

The thinking of Aquinas followed a similar pattern in fundamental areas of his theological anthropology and ethics.[2] It has not been sufficiently noted how the Second Part of the *Summa theologiae* relies on the First Part; that is, how ethics relies on the anthropology of the human person made in the image of God. The Prologue of the First Part of the Second Part intentionally begins with a quotation from John Damascene: the image of God signifies intellect and free will and the capability of acting out of one's own powers. Damascene's lines had concluded a question in the First Part (*ST* I, 93, 9) on the "human person made in the image of God."[3] One could

---

[1] References to *Summa theologiae* (*ST*) are in the text.

[2] See G.de Beaurecueil, *L'homme image de Dieu* (Ottawa, 1951); Guy Lafont, *Structures et méthode dans la Somme théologique de S. Thomas d'Aquin* (Paris, 1961) 265-298.

[3] John Damascene, *De fide orthodoxa* II, ch. 12 (Migne, *Patrolologia Graeca* 94, 962).

continue this consideration by seeing in Aquinas' Christology ways in which people are rendered similar to Christ.[4] What is important is that Aquinas has more and more placed the image of God not in a network of powers and faculties, as St. Augustine did, but in a network of activities (*ST* I, 93, 4 and 7). An image, the likeness in the human person of the Three Persons, is not a static ontological structure. This image of God *realizes itself* in new movements, and that dynamic moves through the totality of the Second Part. God's image is found in formal principles by which the human person journeys to God (the "*movement* of the rational creature towards God" [*ST* I-II, 1]). There is a primacy of activity in relationship to existence, and human existence itself is in act. This is a basic insight of Aquinas' theology. What underlies every movement of human self-realization is a quest for similarity with the Triune God.[5]

More and more I have been struck by the vital importance of eschatology in Aquinas' theology. This eschatology, moreover, seems to have been partly a Christian and theological version of an Aristotelian philosophy of movement. To be a Christian was to be someone moving towards a destiny which was achievement and which brought happiness. "Happiness" here means something quite specific: it is allied to the beatitudes (their title expresses the beatitude of heaven) of the Gospels (*ST* I-II, 69). The beatitudes hold

---

[4] Christ "has shown us a way of truth in himself, a road by which we can arrive at the happiness of immortal life through the resurrection" (*ST* III, prologue; see *ST* I-II, prologue). Parallel themes are the degrees of realization of this image (*ST* I, 93, 4) and degrees of the activities of Christ in us (*ST* III, 8, 3). Also there is the place Aquinas gave to the "*acta et passa Christi*," the insistence (more and more prominent) in his soteriology upon the actions of the Savior so that Christ is for us the way to beatitude because of what he initiated and endured (B. Catao, *Salut et Rédemption chez S. Thomas d'Aquin* (Paris, 1965).

[5] See *Summa contra Gentiles* III, 24.

now and will enjoy completely a future eschatological fruition. This fruition is already partially anticipated in the activity of a life bestowed by virtues and gifts. Beatitude is a wide activity in which all the good acts of the movement of *reditus*, the human movement toward God, end in fullness and fulfillment. That movement is studied in the Second Part and includes all that bestows a just human life.

These observations show that for Thomas Aquinas the human person is a being fashioning itself. The human being realizes itself by its activities—natural and supernatural—under the transcendent God.

II

This conception of the human person realizing its being by activities is particularly present in the teaching of habitus for which Aquinas depends on Aristotle. Habit refers to "having." This having touches the whole human person; it is a having that goes beyond the distinction (one which Gabriel Marcel finds unfortunate) between being and having, a distinction which is so simple that it is a falsification. Etienne Gilson offered an original translation of *habitus* with the French *"ayance,"* "having." A human person fashions itself by its actions.[6] It determines itself through activities but also through modes of having. "A habit bestows a disposition towards something's nature, activity, and destiny" (*ST* I-II, 49, 2, ad 3; I-II, 50, 1 and 2). The human person is not pure act, not totally in act. It can freely orient its self-realization toward good or bad.[7]

Clearly human self-realization requires some duration, some succession of moments; self-realization

---

[6] See *ST* I-II, 51, 2; 52, 3.; *Quaestio disputata de virtutibus in commune* 9.
[7] See *ST* I-II, 49, 4 ad 2; 50, 1 and 3. A habit emerges from the potential quality of the free creature as such to be a power for this or that; this is why there are habits in the angels (*ST* I-II, 50, 6).

needs human time and human history. "The human person according to its nature is not immediately born in such a way that it can attain at once its fullness" (*ST* I, 62, 5 ad 1). Rather, it is natural to the rational person "to arrive from what is incomplete to what is complete by stages" (*ST* I-II, 97, 1). In similar texts Aquinas expresses the historicity of the self-formation of the human person. "Human beings arrive at happiness through time" (*ST* I-II, 5, 1).

Habits are personal and so are the activities they engender. Can one really speak of history if one is talking only about an individual? Was Aquinas thinking of expanding a personal framework? Should we extrapolate what he says about the person and apply it to the totality of the human race? Still, duration is not just the succession of generations as a line of atomized units which add up to a numerical totality but not to a history. We should admit that Aquinas has not developed a historical view of human nature as such. His thought, however, does give access to history.

III

Following Aristotle, Aquinas strongly affirmed the social and political character of the human person.[8] A person realizes human life in society, especially in the realm of the city, the *civitas* which creates, transmits, and displays a "civilization." To fashion a personal self presupposes social life, presupposes an openness to another; there needs to be a docility for receiving from those with whom the riches and realms of a civilization reside. Aquinas linked the social nature of the person to the structure of the human spirit. He knew too that

---

[8] The fact of the generation and multiplication of men and women grounds a kind of infinitude which requires time. "An infinite multitude cannot be actualized all at once but only successively" (*ST* I, 7, 4, ad 1; *ST* III, 8, 3).

when societies move away from insight and lose themselves in the material and the sensual proceeding apart from insight they undergo delays in intellectual progress and pursue directions with dead ends. Clearly in the "common good"—Aquinas made this the object of social activity—the richness of culture occupies a central place. An example of this is the laws acquired by experience which regulate the life of the society. One cannot separate social reality from the historical development of people, and Aquinas discussed this when he discussed habit. My virtue can die with me, but my knowledge largely remains capable of being communicated to others. Aquinas often mentioned the pattern by which a human person (who is simultaneously a corporeal and spiritual being) acts upon another person by the mind (*ST* I, 117) or by the body (*ST* I, 118 and 119). Bodily activity happens through generation involving heredity; spiritual activity happens through *doctrina* with its teaching and examples. If much of our human thinking is strictly personal and dies with us, some ideas, moral convictions, inventions, and creations of culture remain in the libraries and treasuries of society and are transmitted from one generation to another.

This approach of human influences (frequently found in Aquinas' writings[9]) might offer a framework for a historical or social realization of his teaching. A person who comes into this world in the Twentieth Century rather than in the ice age comes into a country, a society, a family with a richer milieu. That person shares in human nature not in an abstract and general way but in a developed format enhanced by many activities and products. The milieu of life in which

---

[9] See the openings of Aristotle's writings on ethics and politics.

someone lives has been extensively thought out and developed by those who have preceded us.¹⁰

Aquinas observed that historical ages are present in what the human race learns about its religious situation.¹¹ His theology in a general way invites us—almost commissions us—to speak of development. "A person is not complete from the very beginning but through a kind of temporal order of successive events, just as a person is first a child and later an adult" (*ST* I-II, 106).¹² Here Aquinas took up a theme dear to St. Augustine: "In this way the succession of human beings during the course of so many centuries must be viewed as one person who ceaselessly exists and continually learns."¹³ Aquinas used this idea to explain original sin (he inevitably cites Porphyry): just as different members of the body are parts of the person of one human being, so all men and women are parts and similar members of human nature. That is why

---

¹⁰ We have touched on this in "Traditio und Sacra Doctrina bei Thomas von Aquin," in Johannes Betz and Heinrich Fries, eds., *Kirche und Überlieferung* (Freiburg, 1960) 170-210.

¹¹ See Yves Congar, "Perspectives chretiennes sur la vie personelle et la vie collective," in *Socialisation et personne humaine* (Lyon, 1960) 195-233.

¹² See Congar, "Le Sens de l'economie salutaire dans la theologiede saint Thomas d'Aquin," in Edwin Iserloh, ed., *Festgabe Joseph Lortz* II (Baden-Baden, 1957) 73-122; Max Seckler, *Das Heil in der Geschichte. Geschichtstheologisches Denken bei Thomas von Aquin* (Munich, 1963). We are not suggesting that Thomas Aquinas originated an appreciation of history; one finds that already with Bernard of Chartres ("*veritas, filia temporis*"); it is also present in Hugh of St. Victor ("*historia dispensationis temporalis divinae providentiae*") and St. Bonaventure (see. J. Ratzinger, *Die Geschichtstheologie des hl. Bonaventura* [Munich, 1959]). See J. Le Goff, *La civilization de l'Occident médiéval* (Paris, 1965) and Henri de Lubac, *L'Exégèse médiéval* II (Paris, 1961) 504-527.

¹³ Augustine, *De vera religione* XXVI, 49; XXVII, 50; *The City of God* 10, 14. Pascal treats this in *Preface sur le Traité du Vide, Oeuvres complètes* I (Paris, 1998) 452-58. The comparison between the ages of the world and the ages of a human person was a theme of pagan antiquity (Paul Archambault, "The Ages of Man and the Ages of the World," *Revue des études augustiniennes* 12 (1966): 193-228.

Porphyry says that by participation "in the species many human beings are one human being."[14] This is only a framework. Thomas did not develop the idea of a lengthy history of the human race, although he recognized it exists. He himself never stopped learning in the school of the ancient theologians, the *sancti*. "*Sacra doctrina*" was the result of the totality of their tradition ceaselessly taken up anew, elaborated, and deepened.[15] People are born forward by previous generations.

IV

Does not Thomas Aquinas offer in his theology, even in the texts we are citing, too abstract and too fixed an idea of human nature and of natural law? Is not his viewpoint (like everything in the Middle Ages) not really historical but cosmological and spatial?[16] Is it not the medieval perspective of a stable panoply of essences arranged in a hierarchical manner? Aquinas, medieval thinkers, and Catholic teaching up through *Humanae vitae* - are they not the heirs of a Stoic concept of a natural law that, because it is the expression of Eternal Reason, will always be fixed, definitively fixed?

We need to mention Stoicism here, although it is wrong to attribute that mentality to Aquinas. He depended on Aristotle whom he tried to harmonize with St. Augustine. With Aristotle nature is the realm of that which the human person can become; nature is a principle giving structure, a principle received through generation. Nature permits an attribution of what is human to all the individuals in the group. Nature is a

---

[14] Aquinas, *In epistolam Sancti Pauli ad Romanos* c. v, lectura 3; see *ST* I-II 81, 1.
[15] See Yves Congar, "Perspectives ...," cited above.
[16] On this aspect, often denounced in a simplistic way see Ratzinger, *Die Geschichtstheologie des hl. Bonaventura*.

principle received by generation. Far from opposing history nature understood in this way includes it. "Human nature is not at work only in one culture. Human nature is not so much an immediate reality as a goal and a reality to be realized. The human person must become that which it is and must become other than it is right now."[17]

Aquinas related natural law to an eternal law which is Divine Reason, but he did not identify the two (as stoicism does). The eternal law which is God remains transcendent. Natural law is an immanent expression created in the creature's knowledge and freedom. From God, from his eternal Law, the human person has received "inclinations to proper activities and goals" by which the person becomes "a participant in divine providence, providing for self and others" (*ST* I-II, 91, 2; see *ST* I, 18, 3). Human beings live not amid a cosmological theory but within a perspective that is anthropological and ultimately historical.[18]

Knowing accurately how Aquinas saw the practical order is useful. God has placed in finite human reason—it is an aspect of our human nature —a share of God's light. Human reason is active; it moves toward God. Everything is not given at once, and so thinking moves "from general principles to particular ideas" (*ST* I-II, 94, 4). When this is viewed *not in an individual but in* a *historical, human group,* a zone of "natural law" emerges, a zone Aquinas designated as that of secondary precepts.[19] A domain of natural law depends upon historical, social, and cultural progress. A Thomist like

---

[17] Pierre Antoine, "Consciences et loi naturelle," *Etudes* 317 (May, 1963): 162-183.

[18] See the helpful views of J. B. Metz, *Christliche Anthropozentrik. Über die Denkform des Thomas von Aquin* (Munich, 1962).

[19] See *ST* I-II, 94, 5 and 6; 104, 3, ad 1; see R. A. Armstrong, *Primary and Secondary Precepts in Thomistic Natural Law Teaching* (The Hague, 1966).

Georges Renard spoke of "natural law with a progressive content," and others (including even Pius XII) have expressed themselves in similar ways.[20] Natural law is a rather large field for historicity. There is a genealogy of natural rights. Thomas Aquinas (citing Aristotle) writes that "human nature is not immutable like divine nature." Thinking of marriage, he added: "That is why even that which is of the natural law diversifies itself according to different states or human conditions" (*ST Supplement*, 41, 1, ad 3).

V

Theologians of the past, Thomas Aquinas among them, looked at the world as a totality. The universe was an ordered, immense totality in which beings live according to a sequence of birth and in which they live with each other through complex interactions and conditions. Today's science, much more precise than medieval knowledge, confirms this view. Creation brings relationships of ontological dependence where all beings are contingent in light of Absolute Being. Creation is not a primal snap of the fingers—an approach Pascal imputed to Descartes. Creation applies to the world in its totality and to as the world as it is at each moment in its history. Creation includes all the coordinates, interactions, and dependent relationships among all the entities within the cosmos as well as developments in economics and culture. The universe is always in the process of becoming in each instant contemporary. The reality of creation includes the world's time and its becoming.

---

[20] See Georges Renard, *L'ordre et la raison* (Paris, 1927); L. Janssens, *Liberté de conscience et liberté religieuse* (Paris, 1964); G. Herberichs, *Théorie de la paix selon Pie XII* (Paris, 1964).

THE HISTORICITY OF THE HUMAN PERSON

Aquinas as a disciple of Aristotle gave time a certain objective reality in which its movement through the activity of the intellect is a measure. Everything created is marked by time's movement; this movement is an aspect of the actuation to which a being aspires. People are concretely determined by the actions in which they fashion themselves. One can say that God creates them according to many historical, cosmic and social relationships; indeed, he creates them for those relationships. In this sense, we could—along with A.-D. Sertillanges who profoundly reflected on Aquinas' idea of creation—accept the idea of Edouard Le Roy. "It seems that the Creator's act sets up the vast length of the duration we observe; it does not so much fashion beings and things by a direct operation as let them fashion themselves."[21] Thomas Aquinas would not have seen any contradiction between the idea of direction and action, for divine direction is of another order than created activities and relationships.

In conclusion, we need to say what we said at the beginning. We have not wanted to make Thomas Aquinas a modern philosopher, a pre-Heideggerian thinker. We do think, however, that we have shown that his thought is not static, rigid, or fixed. His thinking holds sources and aspects for a perspective of human historicity.

---

[21] A. D. Sertillanges, *L'idée de création et ses retentissements en philosophie* (Paris, 1945).

EXPORING THOMAS AQUINAS

Saracens and Thomas Aquinas
Jean-Pierre Torrell, O.P.

Along with pagans and Jews there is a third large category of non-Christians present in the religious world of Thomas Aquinas. We designate them today as Muslims. In his time, they did not have that name. From the Eighth Century on, the word most frequently employed by Christians for followers of Muhammad was "Saracens" (*sarraceni*). In the Twelfth Century, Peter the Venerable—he was the first to translate the Koran into Latin—could write a treatise, Against the Saracens. Thomas himself employed this term twenty-three times in different places, notably in the *Summa contra Gentiles*[1] and in the small work written about the same time, *De rationibus fidei ad Cantorem antiochenum*.[2] That second work's title could be made more explicit by adding, not without reason, *et contra Sarracenos*.

Thomas knew, however, other terms for Muslims. A few times he speaks of Moors in a stereotyped expression as he designates Muslim theologians as "those who speak in the law of the Moors" ("*loquentes in lege maurorum*").[3] Only once does he call them after the name of their prophet Muhammad, "*Mahumetistae*," while he mentions Muhammad four times.[4] On the other hand, Aquinas spoke frequently of "Arabs" who are

---

[1] For instance, *Summa contra Gentiles* [*SCG*] I, 23 ; III, 27; III, 97; IV, 83 [with one or two "r"s].

[2] *De rationibus fidei ad Cantorem antiochenum*, chapters. 1, 7, 8.

[3] *De veritate* q. 5 a. 9 ad 4; *SCG* III, 65; III, 69; *De potentia* q. 3 a. 7. The *Index Thomisticus* mentions a fifth and sixth usage, but these are from an inauthentic passage and from an apocryphal opusculum. The expression in *lege maurorum* has its doublet with *in lege sarracenorum* (*SCG* I, 23; *SCG* III, 97).

[4] "Mahumetistae" in *SCG* I, 2; "Mahumetus" in *In Psalm.* 2; *SCG* I, 6; *In Epistolam I ad Corinthios* 15, 1, lectura 1; *Summa theologiae* (*ST*) II-II, 12, 1 ad 2.

mentioned forty times. Most often this occurs in a geographical sense (as in his biblical commentaries) but more than ten times he uses "Arabs" or the singular "Arab" to mean philosophers representing various opinions, views different from those of Greek philosophers.[5]

Let us look at the historical context of Aquinas' usage. In contrast to the Jews with whom Christians had learned to live together for centuries in the same territorial areas (even if the relationships were not always peaceful), the Saracens in the Thirteenth Century represented a danger threatening Christianity from outside (it will take more than two hundred more years before they are completely driven out of Spain). They had a bad reputation: for centuries, the populations around the Mediterranean lived in fear of "*razzias*" conducted by pirates who not only pillaged towns but seized people to make them slaves. In the Thirteenth Century, the situation is not much better. For a brief time in the kingdoms of the Near East, Christians and Muslims developed a certain cohabitation, but the Arab re-conquest placed this fragile equilibrium in question, and the taking of Jerusalem by the Saracens in 1244 led Louis IX to try a seventh crusade. That turned out badly, and the venture did not block the loss of Antioch in 1268.

For Thomas Aquinas, these are contemporary events and they touch him as a theologian and as a Dominican. They involve him as a theologian when two or three years before the fall of Antioch a dignitary in

---

[5] See *SCG* II, 79. That citation and one in *De articulis fidei* [I, 6] from Gennadius of Marseille's *Liber Ecclesiasticorum dogmatum* uses the Latin singular "*arabi*"; see also *De veritate* q. 14 a. 1; *De spiritualibus creaturis* a. 9 ad 6; *De unitate intellectus*, chapter 2, 5; *Super librum de causis, proemium*.

that church wrote to him to inquire about questions often posed to Christians by Saracens concerning topics in their faith. Aquinas knew the difficulties of his Dominican confreres in those regions. Already in 1228 there was a Dominican province of the Holy Land, and the leaders of the Order spoke about it frequently in their letters, letters seeking vocations for that province and encouraging the study of languages. In 1256, a letter of the Master of the Dominican Order Humbert of Romans ended with information that in that same year two friars had been killed by pagans and two others decapitated by Saracens. A little later, in 1268, there are five Dominicans (one was the vicar of the patriarch of Antioch) who were executed when Antioch was captured by Sultan Baybars.[6]

Without going into historical detail, one can think that those events did not favor a balanced judgment. Possibly Thomas was unconsciously influenced by that situation, although information about this world is not clearly evident in passages where he speaks of Saracens and their religion. He used different sources. There is no doubt that he knew well Arab philosophy, for instance, Avicenna and Averroes whom he cited hundreds of times[7] as he did with the Jew Maimonides. He discussed with them as with equals; he may have disagreed with them strongly but he recognized their high intellectual

---

[6] See Humbertus de Romanis, *Opera de vita regulari*, J.-J. Berthier ed. (Rome, 1889) II, 500-504; see B. Altaner, *Die Dominikanermissionen des 13. Jahrhunderts* (Habelschwerdt, 1924).

[7] Let us recall some numbers: there are 405 citations of Avicenna, 503 citations of Averroes, 205 citations of other Arab and Jewish authors (of which eighty-two are of Maimonides); see C. Vansteenkiste, "Avicenna-Citaten bij S. Thomas", *Tijdschrift voor Philosophie* 15 (1953): 457-507; "San Tommaso d'Aquino ed Averroè", *Rivista degli Studi Orientali* 32 (1957): 585-623; "Autori Arabi e Giudei nell'opera di San Tommaso", *Angelicum* 37 (1960): 336-401. R. Imbach, "Alcune precisazioni sulla presenza di Maimonide in Tommaso d'Aquino," *Studi 1995, N.S.* 2 (Rome, 1995): 48-64.

level. He was, however, not much concerned with their faith, their religious beliefs. He was not at all interested in aspects that interest us like concrete knowledge of their religion or its cultural milieu. Still, Thomas would not have had access to much information about culture and religion. Specialists think it is unlikely that he had much possibility of having direct contact with that world. Furthermore, he did not show the slightest curiosity about the contemporary context of Islam. He seems never to have made any effort to read the Koran although there were two Latin translations available in his time.[8] If some of his writings show a general, oblique knowledge, even this comes unfortunately from second hand and tendentious sources, from Christian refutations of Muslim errors.[9]

Certainly, Thomas recognized at times that Christians, Jews, and Saracens worshipped God and that they all, for instance, confessed his omnipotence[10] and unity.[11] Still, there is at least one passage where he

---

[8] The oldest and the most widely known is the translation made by Peter the Venerable (R. Glei, ed., *Petrus Venerabilis, Schriften zum Islam* (Altenberge, 1985); see J.-P. Torrell and D. Bouthillier, *Pierre le Vénérable et sa vision du monde* (Louvain, 1986) 180-195; J.-P. Torrell, "La notion de prophétie et la méthode apologétique dans le Contra Saracenos de Pierre le Vénérable," *Studia monastica* 17 (1975): 257-282.

[9] See Louis Gardet, "La connaissance que Thomas d'Aquin put avoir du monde islamique", in G. Verbeke and D. Verhelste, eds., *Aquinas and the Problems of His Time* (The Hague, 1976) 139-149; "Saint Thomas et ses prédécesseurs arabes", in *St. Thomas Aquinas : 1274-1974. Commemorative Studies*, I (Toronto, 1974) 419-448; R.-A. Gauthier. "Introduction", *Saint Thomas d'Aquin, Somme contre les Gentils* (Paris, 1993).

[10] *De rationibus fidei...*, ch. 7 and ch. 8.

[11] *Super primam Decretalem.*

makes the Saracens equal to pagans,[12] and there is the one passage in the *Summa contra Gentiles* which treats the religion of the Muslims in a quite pejorative way. The goal of Thomas' argument there is to show the different ways in which Christianity and Islam have expanded throughout the world. "The point is clear in the case of Muhammad. He seduced people by promises of carnal pleasure to which the concupiscence of the flesh goads us."[13] This argument uses a literal reading of texts from Islam and is repeated later in the *Summa contra Gentiles* as he mentions a paradise of earthly delights. Elsewhere he places Jews in the same limited position as the Saracens.[14] The precepts of Muslims "were in conformity with his promises and gave free rein to carnal pleasure." "Precepts" here probably means the Koran. Peter the Venerable spoke of a "*collectio praeceptorum*." "As for proofs of his doctrine, he brought forward only such as could be grasped by the natural ability of someone with a very modest wisdom. Indeed, the truths that he taught were mingled with fables and doctrines of the greatest falsity." In the *Summa contra Gentiles*, Aquinas seems to forget that among the truths taught by Muhammad there are truths of some significance like monotheism. "He did not bring forth

---

[12] Christians can have as servants infidels, Jews, pagans, and Saracens (*ST* II-II, 10, 9 ad 3). Here Thomas did not treat fully this objection and said little about it in his response. On the other hand, one does not find with him the tendency to consider Islam as a Christian heresy, a topic Peter the Venerable explicitly pursued (see J.-P. Torrell and D. Bouthillier, *Pierre le Vénérable et sa vision du monde*, 189, 334-339) as did Anselm of Canterbury, Abelard, and Alain de Lille.

[13] The following quotations are from *SCG* I, 6.

[14] "The fables of the Jews and Sarracens are rejected because they find the reward of the just in pleasures" (*SCG* III, 27). "The error of the Jews and the Sarracens must be rejected because they emphasize in the resurrection people drinking and eating as they do now. That view was also followed by some Christian heretics" (*SCG* IV, 83). See Peter the Venerable, *Summa totius haeresis Sarracenorum* n° 9, in *Petrus Venerabilis, Schriften* 10-12.

any signs produced in a supernatural way, which alone fittingly gives witness to divine inspiration." Here Thomas is clearly thinking of miracles and of different signs performed by the Apostles at the time of the first preaching of the Gospel (see *Letter to the Hebrews* 2, 4). A hundred years before, Peter the Venerable also had been disturbed by an absence of miracles in Islam.[15] In place of seeking the support of miracles, "[Muhammad] said that he was sent by the power of arms: those signs, however, are also present in robbers and tyrants." Thomas continued: "Those who believed in him were brutal men and desert wanderers, utterly ignorant of all divine teaching, and through their numbers Muhammad forced others to become his followers by the violence of arms."

It is painful to find this kind of argumentation coming from Aquinas' pen. He did not recognize in his argument the very description given of the first Christians as "people without education or culture" (*Acts of the Apostles* 4, 15) or the ridicule used later by Celsus: "workers, farmers, painters, people utterly uncultured and vulgar."[16] Thomas continued: "Nor do divine pronouncements on the part of preceding prophets offer him any witnesses. On the contrary, he perverts almost all the testimonies of the Old and New Testament by making them into fabrications of his own." His followers do not see any problems here in that he has forbidden them to read the Christian Scriptures, asserting that there what is true is mixed with what is false. If the Koran gives at times a distorted presentation of the Bible (one wonders what was the exact source for this biblical information), Muhammad never formally

---

[15] See D. Bouthillier and J.-P. Torrell, "Miraculum. Une catégorie fondamentale chez Pierre le Vénérable", *Revue Thomiste* 80 (1980): 378-81.

[16] See R.-A. Gauthier, "Introduction," 126.

forbade his followers to read the Bible. He encouraged discussions with non-believers. Finally, Thomas concludes, the Saracens follow the word of a man guaranteed neither by miracles nor by prophecies attesting to its divine origin. "It is clear that those who join his faith through these words find believing something easy."

Aquinas' understanding of the religion left to his followers by Muhammad shows no sympathy toward Islam. Clearly, if the author had had the least interest in this religion he would have learned more about it by reading the Koran itself and he would have learned how to express with more nuance its teaching and its historical figures. The actual source for Aquinas' viewpoints—this has been known for a long time—is the Risâla ("*Apology*") of Pseudo-al-Kindi, an Arab Christian from the Ninth or Tenth Century, a text which Peter the Venerable had translated into Latin at the same time as he translated the Koran. That work is made up of two letters. The first shorter one of fifteen pages is written by a Muslim inviting a Christian to convert to Islam. The other, longer, is the answer of this Christian (who calls himself al-Kindi) inviting the Muslim to join the Christian faith and giving objections to the teaching of Muhammad. This second letter is the work of someone who lived in Bagdad amid Muslims. A work of accurate information, it is a text of religious apologetics. It contains the main themes of Christian apologetics directed against Islam as it will subsequently develop. This detailed exposition may have been an excuse for Aquinas not to do any further research on Islam. Regardless, the fact that he was content with this text shows—contrary to what was long thought—that Islam was not a preoccupation or an interest when he wrote the *Summa contra Gentiles*.[17]

There is, however, a second discussion by Thomas Aquinas of Saracens on religion. It is in the small work entitled, *De rationibus fidei ad Cantorem antiochenum*. This book is a response to someone whose name is not given but who has the title of "Cantor" of the church of Antioch. He posed to Aquinas a number of questions on difficulties encountered by Christians in that cosmopolitan city. Some, touching on eschatology, were raised by Greek and Armenian Christians. The ones coming from the Saracens interest us, and they touch on two important points: faith in the son of God, and human free will. We can set aside the second point but it is worth reading some of his ideas on the first.

> The Saracens, as you say, ridicule our claim that Christ is the Son of God, since God does not have a wife; and, assuming that we profess there are three gods, they think us mad. They also mock our belief that Christ, the Son of God, was crucified for the salvation of the human race, because if God is omnipotent, he could have saved the human race without the suffering of his own Son He could also have so constructed man that he would not have sinned. They rebuke Christians because daily at the altar they eat their God and because the body of Christ, were it

---

[17] An edition of the Risâla is in J. Muñoz Sendino, "Al-Kindi : Apologia del Cristianismo," *Miscellanea Comillas* 11-12 (1949): 337-460. The author is referred to as Pseudo-al-Kindi to avoid confusing him with the great philosopher with the same Arab name who lived from 795 to 865. On this text and Aquinas' use of it see S. Van Riet, "La Somme contre les Gentils et la polémique islamo-chrétienne," *Aquinas and the Problems of His Time*, 150-160 ; for comments and a bibliography see Gauthier, "Introduction," 119-127.

as big as a mountain, should long since have been consumed.[18]

It is instructive to read this text immediately after reading the passage we cited from the *Summa contra Gentiles*. The context has reversed itself completely; mockery has changed sides. The Saracens give the Christians the same kind of sarcasm that they have received. The change in style is significant. Thomas took the issues seriously; in several responses he advised the Cantor in Antioch not to open himself to ridicule by pretending to be able to prove the truths of faith by reasons which in fact don't exist.[19] If the content of Aquinas' response is worth being better known, it is its "tonality" that interests us. Not every polemical point has disappeared, but gone is the emotional tone present in the *SCG* when he replied briskly to objection after objection, objections inadequate for a real philosophical and theological discussion.[20] The response lacks impatience and develops speculation at a high level on the Incarnation, the Trinity, and free will. The exposition is rather precise, the language simple. When he speaks of Christ in his passion and his choice of a poor and

---

[18] *De rationibus fidei...*, chap. 1; see Gilles Emery's introduction and notes in Traités. *Les raisons de la foi. Les articles de foi et les sacrements de l'Église* (Paris, 1999); J. Ellul, "Thomas Aquinas and Muslim-Christian Dialogue. An Appraisal of *De rationibus fidei*," *Angelicum* 80 (2003): 177-200. In English there is Thomas Aquinas, *On Reasons for Our Faith against the Muslims, Greeks and Armenians* [translation by Peter Damian Fehlner] (New Bedford, 2002). Joseph Kenny's translation with a "Foreword" can be found in *Islamochristiana* 21 (1996): 31-50.

[19] See Emery's introduction to De rationibus fidei..., 26-27.

[20] "(Their) mockery of God is itself ridiculous. Their sensuality keeps them from conceiving anything beyond flesh and blood" (*On Reasons for our Faith against the Muslims, Greeks and Armenians*, ch. 3). Their manner of deriding the passion of Christ comes from "a blindness of spirit incapable of grasping the depths of so great a mystery" (ch. 5). "The derision by the infidels of the sacrament [the Eucharist] is quite empty" (ch. 8).

despised life, one can say that he expresses himself with some emotion, almost turning the pages into a kind of personal confession of faith. One senses that Thomas was affected by these mockeries in Antioch, but he did not respond in his earlier tone. He developed an apologetic of a high quality, removed from the inferior arguments echoed in the *Summa contra Gentiles*. He did not unfold here the kind of argumentation that he would with regards to the Jews, because the Saracens do not admit the revealed Bible. He remained on the terrain of natural reason. Because the truths of faith cannot be proven (faith is beyond human reason), he worked at defending what faith believes and at showing "with reasons that what the Catholic faith confesses is not false."[21]

---

[21] *De rationibus fidei*..., ch. 2.

Thomas Aquinas' Theology of the Church

Yves Congar, O.P.

Thomas Aquinas (1225-1274) did not write a special treatise on the church although recent books and articles do not let us doubt that he had a conception of the church that was both precise and rich. Sometimes these studies on his ecclesiological thought highlight interesting details; other times they just recall texts on topics where Thomas has no originality.[1] Here we want to try to extract what is present and to give it an expression that is if not completely new at least more distinctive and personal. Thomas Aquinas had, in our view, a perspective that is tied to his conception of theology, one that is linked to the theological virtues like faith. The church touches on a communion with the

---

[1] See J. Bainvel, "L'idée de l'Église au Moyen Age," *La Science catholique* 4 (1899): 975-988; M. Grabmann, *Die Lehre des hl. Thomas von Aquin von der Kirche als Gotteswerk* (Regensburg, 1903); J. Geiselmann, "Christus u. die Kirche nach Thomas von Aquin," *Theologische Quartalschrift* 107 (1926): 198-222; T. Kaeppeli, *Zur Lehre des hl. Thomas vom Aquin vom Corpus Christi mysticum* (Paderborn, 1931); M.-J. Congar, "L'Idée thomiste de l'Église," *Esquisses du mystère de l'Église* (Paris, 1941) 59-91; "L'Apostolicité de l'Église selon saint Thomas d'Aquin," *Revue des sciences philosophiques et théologiques* 44 (1927): 233-255; T. Kaeppeli, *Zur Lehre des hl. Thomas von Aquin* (1960): 209-224; A. Darquennes, "La definition de l'Église d'après saint Thomas d'Aquin," *L'Organisation corporative du Moyen Âge à la fin de l'Ancien Régime* (Louvain, 1943) 1-53; *De juridische Structuur van de Kerk volgens S. Th. van Aq.* (Louvain, 1949); E. Vauthier, "Le Saint-Esprit, principe d'unité de l'Église d'après saint Thomas d'Aquin," *Mélanges de science religieuse* 5 (1948): 175-196; 6 (1949): 57- 80; A. Mitterer, *Geheimnisvoller Leib Christi nach St. Thomas von Aquin und nach Papst Pius XII* (Vienna, 1950); M. Useros Carretero, *"Statuta Ecclesiae" y "Sacramenta Ecclesiae" en la eclesiologia de S. Tomas* (Rome, 1962); M.-J. Le Guillou, *Le Christ et l'Église, Théologie du mystère* (Paris, 1963); M. Seckler, *Das Heil in der Geschichte. Geschichtstheologisches Denken bei Thomas von Aquin* (Munich, 1964) (cited according to the French translation of 1967).

mystery of God in his divinity. The church in its most profound reality, a reality that includes a broad extension and a lengthy span, is the divinizing community with God. In our earthly situation, however, with flesh and history, this is realized first in Christ, the incarnate word, and then through what he employs to sustain us: faith, sacraments, institutions.[2] That is why, although there is only one church, it is necessary to speak of it in two ways. On can and must distinguish in the church two registers of common life and law, two criteria of hierarchy.

The church is functionally and principally union with God: in heaven through glory and vision and here below through grace and faith. Grace is the seed of glory, and faith is the seed of vision. There is a unity in the principle of existence between agents and "those comprehending" (the church of heaven), and the faithful or the church on earth.[3] This is the strong meaning that

---

[2] On this group of realities see *ST* I-II, 106, 1, 2; 107, 1, ad 2 and ad 3; 111, 1, a. 5 ad 1; *ST* III, 63, 1, ad 1 and ad 3; L. B. Gillon, "L'imitation du Christ et la morale de saint Thomas," *Angelicum* 36 (1959): 263-286. On how Thomas explains the distinction between sanctifying grace and grace gratis data see the commentary on Romans, c. 1, lect. 1; *In IV Sent.*, d. 24, q. 1, a. 1, qu. 1, ad 3 and ad 2; qu. 1, ad 2 and ad 3. On the distinction of the two forums and two excommunications (see *In IV Sent*, d. 19, q. 1, a. 1, sol. 3); on the two hierarchies of holiness and of function see *IV Sent.*, d. 24, q. 1, a. 1, qu. 1, ad 3; *Questiones disputatae de spiritualibus creaturis* 8, ad 11; *ST* II-II, 184, 4; *De perfectione vitae spiritualis*, chapters 23, 24 citing the passage "every prelature will cease" from the *Glossa ordinaria* (PL 113, 547); Peter Lombard, *In II Sent.*, d. 6, c. 4. The sacraments are related "to the worship of the church at the present time" (*ST* III, 63, 1, ad 1; 3, ad 3; 5, ad 3) and they will cease (*ST* III, 61, 4, ad 1; 63, 5 ad 3). Just as Christ is the "way of arriving at godliness" (*Compendium theologiae* II, 3; *ST* I-II, prologue; *ST* III, prologue), so the "church militant is on a journey to be the church triumphant" (*In IV Sent.*, d. 18, q. 2, a. 3).

[3] The grace of the present time (which because of that grace is "the ultimate age") is functionally the same as that of glory (*De Veritate* 27, 5, ad 6; *ST* I-II, 111, 3, ad 2). Faith is "that by which eternal life is begun in us" (*ST* II-II, 4, 1) and grace is a principle of formation in godliness (*De Virtutibus in commune* 1, 2, ad 21; *ST* II-II, 19, 7).

Thomas gave to the formula "*Ecclesia* equals *congregatio* (*coetus*, *collection*, *universitas*, *societas*, *collegium*) *fidelium*," a formula used frequently in various periods of the church but which here expresses a definition of the church.[4] The expression has a theological reference and not a socio-political one. This church encompasses all those who believe in Christ, whether from the past or from the future. This is the theme of the church from the time of Abel or that of the universal church.[5] So the church is seen as the ensemble or supernatural unity of persons vivified by the grace of God; in short, it is seen as a work or effect of grace.[6] Related to Christ as to its measure, sovereign, principle, nd standard, this work of grace merits essentially the name of Body of Christ. That is why Aquinas conceived the Mystical Body to be first simply the society of the saints without including there the aspect of visibility or hierarchical structure.[7] Ultimately when the approach is that of human beings one can say that the church, seen one more time at this level, encompasses the total return toward God, that is to say, the entire *Secunda Pars* of the *Summa theologiae*.[8]

There are several principles of unity in the church that exist permanently at the profound level of its being.

---

[4] See Darquennes, *La Definition* 8-22; Seckler, 209 (note 24); some references in Aquinas to this point are *In IV Sent.*, d. 20, q. 1, a. 4, sol. 1; *De Veritate* 29, 4; *Summa contra Gentes* IV, 78; *ST* I, 117, 2, ad 1; *ST* III, 8, 4, ad 2; the commentaries on *First Corinthians* (chapter 12, lect. 3) and *Hebrews* (chapter 3, lect. 1), and the commentary on the Creed (a. 9).

[5] On the church from Abel on, see *ST* III, 8, 3. There is only one church of the just including those mentioned in the Old Testament and Christians (*In III Sent.*, d. 19, a. 1, sol. 2; *De Veritate* 14, 12; 29,7 ad 7; *ST* I-II, 106, 1 ad 3; *ST* II-II, 2, 7; 98, 2, ad 4; *ST* III, 8, 3, ad 3; 68, 1; commentary on the Creed (1. 9); for both topics see Seckler.

[6] *In III Sent.*, d. 25, q. 1, a. 2, ad 10; *De Veritate* 29, 5.

[7] "The society of the holy" (*ST* III, 80, 4) of which the angels are a part (*ST* III, 8, 4).

[8] See Congar, "L'Idée thomiste."

In the entitative order there is a plan of being whose specific unity is that of grace. In an intentional plan, that is, in the actualizing form of intelligence and will, the numerical unity comes from God himself. Going further, while God himself (and by appropriation the Holy Spirit) dwells fully in and animates all the saints, this activity begins with the humanity of Christ. The formed members of the Body-Church of Christ "have for their ultimate principle of achievement that which is identically the same in all."[9] Thus the Holy Spirit is the ultimate principle of the unity of the church.[10] One must insist, however, that Thomas did not develop this aspect in any detail, although his theology of grace as a created habit does lead in a dominant and frequent way to consider Christ as communicating grace to others.

Thomas joins himself to a significant tradition ("as the saints say") that has seen the earthly church drawing its existence form the passion of Christ. "From the side of Christ dead on the cross the sacraments have flowed forth, that is the blood and water by which the church is made."[11] His originality lies in having introduced the idea of an instrumental causality for the humanity of

---

[9] *In III Sent*, d. 13, q. 2, a. 2, sol. 2; *Compendium theologiae* I, 147. See observations on Vauthier's "Le Saint-Esprit..." and other writings mentioned in Congar, "Chronique: Année 1953," *Sainte Église* (Paris, 1963) 647-49. Thomas distributed the different roles of the Holy Spirit and of Christ according to analogies with the heart and head (*ST* III, 8, 1, ad 3). According to Grabmann, Thomas was the first to make the Holy Spirit to be the heart of the mystical body.

[10] *ST* II-II, 183, 3, ad 3.

[11] "From the side of Christ dead on the cross the sacraments flowed, that is, blood and water, from which the church is instituted" (*ST* I, 92, 3; *ST* III, 64, 2, ad 3; *In IV Sent.*, d. 3, q. 1, a. 3, sol. 2). See too the statement: "The church is founded on faith and on the sacraments of faith" (*In IV Sent.*, d. 17, q. 3, a. 1, sol. 5; d. 27, q. 3, a. 3, ad 2); similar phrases are "constituted," "made by" (*ST* III, 64, 2, ad 3), "instituted" (*ST* I, 92, 3), and "consecrated" (*In Joannis*, 19, lect. 5, # 4). "The church is one through a unity of faith and sacraments" (*In Joannis* 6., lect. 3; *Quaestio quodlibetalis* XII, 19).

Christ into the theology of Christ the head.[12] The church militant is on the way toward that of the blessed where it is totally dependent on Christ, also constitutes its head. All the benefits of grace are realized in Christ:[13] men and women become participants of grace and as such are members of the church, members by faith and by the sacraments of faith.[14] These come to them through ministries and forms partly instituted by Christ and partly determined by the church itself. Aquinas has some views and statements on the church precisely as an institution of salvation and on the church as a community of believers: it is the same church.[15] Setting aside those that are common to him and theologians of his time, let us focus briefly on aspects that are more original and personal, six basic perspectives concerning the institution of the church.

1. In his very rich theology of the sacraments Thomas placed the Eucharist at the center or at the summit. Containing Christ himself, it contains all the benefits offered to the entire church.[16] Thomas identified the presbyteral

---

[12] See Theophil Tschipke, *Die Menschheit Christi als Heilsorgan der Gottheit unter besonderer Berüchsichtigung der Lehre des hl. Thomas von Aquin* (Freiburg, 1940). Aquinas owes this idea less to the philosophy of Aristotle than to the Greek Fathers like Cyril of Alexandria and John Damascene; see I. Backes, *Die Christologie des Thomas von Aquin und die griechischen Väter* (Paderborn, 1931) 241-47, 270-86. The theme appears in questions 27 to 29 of *De Veritate*.

[13] *In IV Sent.*, d. 49, q. 4, a. 3, ad 4; see *De Veritate* 29, 5; *ST* III, 7, 9; 24, 3 and 4; the commentary on the Creed, a. 10.

[14] *De Veritate* 27, 4; 29, 7, ad 8. Aquinas is not the only one to see the sacraments as the consequence of the Incarnation.

[15] See Useros Carretero *"Statuta Ecclesiae" y "Sacramenta Ecclesiae"* and Darquennes, *De juridische*.

[16] "The common spiritual good of the entire church is contained substantially in the very sacrament of the Eucharist" (*ST* III, 66, 3, ad 1; 79, 1). On the Eucharist and the "unity of the mystical body" see *In IV Sent*, d. 8, q. 2, a. 2; the Eucharist is "the goal of all offices" (*ST* III, 65, 3, 2).

priesthood with "the spiritual power" of consecrating the Eucharist.[17] The climactic sacrament of orders is a "potestative whole" encompassing seven stages (a sacramentality of the "minor orders"). From Etienne d'Autun on,[18] the handing on of the instruments, the chalice and paten, with its accompanying formula are considered the matter and form of the sacrament. That teaching followed by St. Thomas, particularly in the *De articulis fidei et ecclesiae sacramentis*, will be prominent up to the *Decree for the Armenians* at the Council of Florence.[19] Along with other scholastics he saw "the power over the mystical body" to be derived for a priest from his "power over the true body of Christ."[20] The priesthood includes in itself a power aiming at preparing the faithful for the good reception of the Eucharist; when it is a question of preaching, this power cannot pass into actualization without a canonical mission; or, if you are talking about the power of the keys, without jurisdiction.[21] So the priesthood does surpass the simple power of cult in consecrating the Eucharist.

---

[17] *In IV Sent.*, d. 24, q. 1, a. 1, qu 2; q. 2, a. 1.

[18] *Tractatus de sacramento altaris* ch. 6 (*Patrologia Latina* 172, 1281) written between 1170 and 1186.

[19] *Denziger-Schönmetzer* (Freiburg i. Br., 1965) 3126.

[20] *In IV Sent.*, d. 7, q. 3, ad 1; d. 18, q. 1, a. 1; d. 24, q. 1, a. 3, sol. 5; *Summa contra Gentes* IV, 74 and 75; *ST* III, 82, 1.

[21] M. Peuchmaurd, "Mission canonique et prédication," *Recherches de Théologie Ancienne et Médiévale* 30 (1963): 122-144, 251-276. The power of the keys equals priestly character according to *In IV Sent.*, d. 18, q. 1, a. 3, ad 1; see Ulrich Horst, "Das Wesen der 'potestas clavium' nach Thomas von Aquin," *Münchener Theologische Zeitschrift* 11 (1960): 191-201; on an apostolic conception of the priesthood see Le Guillou, 243.

2. Separating himself from the theological current that refers the character of the baptized and the character of the confirmed to their "state given by faith" (Albert, Bonaventure), Thomas saw in baptism and confirmation a participation in the priesthood of Christ and in the power of worship (active and receptive) relative to the worship of the gathered church.[22]

3. Thomas shared the common opinion that the episcopate is more than an office or a simple source of jurisdiction. The episcopacy is also less than a particular degree of the sacrament of orders. Not just a *dignitas*, it is a hierarchical order relative to the mystical body conferred by a consecration that cannot be lost. Under the influence of Psuedo-Denys and patristic texts employed by Gratian, Thomas removed himself from the position of Peter Lombard and approached more and more the view that the episcopate is a kind of principate in the priesthood, an apostolic priesthood.[23]

4. In the area of the historical development of papal authority, Thomas did not in fact have that originality sometimes attributed to him (whether to blame him or to praise him according to the viewpoints of Döllinger, Harnack, and Sohm). In terms of papal authority three points should be noted.

    a. When Thomas (along with other major scholastic thinkers) said that the bishops receive their jurisdiction from

---

[22] *ST* III, 63, 1, 3.
[23] See J. Lécuyer, "Les étapes de l'enseignement thomiste sur l'épiscopat," *Revue Thomiste* 57 (1957): 29-53.

the pope it is necessary to recall that this does not mean the power, "*potestas*," of the priesthood in terms of the episcopacy—this is sacramental—but a designation of subjects, that is, of precisely determined recipients.[24] As the keys (their power and knowledge) must derive from Peter and move to the other apostles, so that power flows from the pope to the bishops.[25] But in which sense? It is not a question of the sacramental power itself but of its employment. One returns to "jurisdiction" to the determination of different degrees of prelature (as a number of texts explain). With regards to the fullness of power, Thomas located it in the ecclesiastical and not in the temporal order. It means a universal quality of episcopal power extending from on high to more things than does the power of each bishop in his diocese or in his province.[26] One cannot at all attribute to Aquinas the idea of episcopal collegiality.

b. The *Contra Errores Graecorum* of 1263 employs inauthentic texts of the Greek Fathers coming from a *Libellus*

---

[24] See *In IV Sent.*, d. 19, q. 1, a. 2, qu. 3 and ad 3, sol. 1; J. Lecuyer, *L'Episcopat et l'Église universelle* (Paris, 1962) 803ff.

[25] See *In II Sent*, d. 44; *In IV Sent.*, d. 18, q. 2, a. 2; d. 20, a. 4, sol. 3; d. 24, q. 3, a. 2 , qu.3, ad 1; *Summa contra Gentes* 4, 72, 76.

[26] In *Contra impugnantes* (c. 4) papal power equals universal episcopal power. The pope is the "the highest of the bishops" and "the first and highest of all bishops" (*In IV Sent.*, d. 7, q. 3, a. 1, ad 3; see d. 20, q. 1, a. 4, sol. 3; d. 25, q. 1, a. 1, ad 3; *Quaestio Quodlibetalis* IV, 13; *ST* II-II, 89, 9, ad 3; *ST* III, 72, 11, ad 1).

composed toward 1254-1256 by Nicolas of Cotrone for the emperor Theodore II Lascaris and about which Pope Urban IV asked Thomas for his opinion.[27] A number of texts, in particular those claiming to be from Saint Cyril of Alexandria, support theses on the papal primacy of jurisdiction and of magisterium. Those texts were cited later at the Council of Florence and then again by Bellarmine.

c. The *Contra Errores Graecorum* argues that it belongs to the pope "to define those things that are of faith."[28] This thesis is taken up in the *Summa theologiae* (a text of great importance for the future of ecclesiology).[29] Thomas took his point of departure from the classic thesis: the ecclesia is not able to err in the area of faith.[30] But its structure is such that it is subject to the pope and his determinations, for major situation and the calling of general councils in

---

[27] See the critical edition by H. Dondaine (Rome, 1967); one should note that Thomas no more used the *Libellus* after composing the *De Potentia* and never in the *Summa theologiae*. Did he, quite possibly, have doubts about its authenticity?

[28] Chapter II, 36.

[29] *ST* II-II, 1, 10.

[30] See *Quaestio Quodlibetalis* IX 16: *ST* II-II 1, 1, sed contra. In *ST* II-II, 2, 6, ad 3 the passage of Luke 22:32 is applied to the "*Universalis ecclesia.*" The same viewpoint is found in Albert (*In IV Sent.*, d. 20, a. 17, 4) and Bonaventure (*In IV Sent.*, d. 20, sole article, 1. 2).

general are referred to him.[31] The pope then is the supreme authority in the area of doctrine. Thomas did not go beyond this, although some will invoke his statement as favoring papal infallibility. One sees how the theology of Nicolas I and that of the *False Decretals* on the role of the pope in the councils find here approval and blessing.

5. One of the most original and remarkable chapters in Aquinas' theology is that of the New Law. There one finds the ground of the degrees of ecclesiological values and the global statute of the institution of the church in itself.[32] "That which is most basic and most powerful in the New Law is the grace of the Holy Spirit... Nevertheless, there are things that dispose one to the grace of the Holy Spirit or pertain to the employment of the Holy Spirit."[33] These "secondary elements" include external means like the letter of the Scripture, the rites of the sacraments, laws, and organization. It is not that Thomas dreamt of a totally spiritual church, for

---

[31] Canon law enters into dogmatic theology with the principle, "the pope is to be judged by no one" (Bonaventure, *De perfectione evangelica*, q. 4, a. 3, 12). On the pope and the councils see Aquinas *In I Sent.*, d. 11, q. 1, a. 1, ad 2; I, 36, ad 2; *ST* II-II, q. 11, a. 2, ad 3; *De Potentia* 10, 4, ad 13; *Contra impugnantes* c. 4.

[32] *ST* I-II, 106, 1 and 2; 107 1 and 4; 108, 1- 3; *ST* III, 42, 4, ad 2; *Commentary on Romans*, 8, lect. 1; *On Hebrews*, 8, lect. 3. Quaestio Quodlibetalis IV, 13); other references can be found in Useros Carretero, 230. The main source of this, after the New Testament, is Augustine, *De spiritu et littera*; Alexander of Hales wrote a similar treatise, De lege evangelica. Thomas employed the famous text by Urban II (Gratian 1 c. XIX, q. 2, col. 839f.): "Private law (from the Holy Spirit is more worthy than public law (from canon law)"; see I. T. Eschmann, "*Bonum commune melius est quam bonum unius,*" *Medieval Studies* 6 [1944]: 100-115.

[33] *ST* I-II, 106, 1.

the church -- grace in its own forms – has in the state of its journey a status of Incarnation.[34] Nevertheless, the evangelism of the friar preacher shows itself here in a direction that will subsequently be rather poorly followed.

6. To turn to the external structures or the organization of the social body that is the church is to see that Thomas had a perspective that is quite pyramidical. The embodiment of the Body of Christ moves from the parish to the universal church passing through the deanery, the diocese, and the province. These concepts are related to ideas about a corporation from the Middle Ages. Thomas did not follow the secular masters who saw the authority of the universal church broken off into pieces and given to the provinces and then to the diocese and from there to the archdiaconates and their parishes.[35] That approach gave to each degree of authority an independence in its own domain. Thomas, however, reestablished the hierarchical structure in favor of the bishops and the pope.

In the area of relationships between the temporal and the spiritual orders, Thomas was quite original in the principles that he had set forth. Still, they too reflected certain views of his time. He had benefited from the arrival of the *Ethics* and in 1260 of the *Politics of Aristotle*.[36] The very word (and even more the

---

[34] See Seckler, 228ff.

[35] See Darquennes, *De juridische Structuur*, 69ff.

[36] See Grabmann, "Das Naturrecht der Scholastik von Gratian bis Thomas von Aquin," *Mittelalterliches Geistesleben* (Munich, 1926) 65ff.; "Studien über den Einfluss der aristotelischen Philosophie auf die mittelalterliche Theorie über das Verhältnis von Staat and Kirche," *Sitzungsberichte der Bayerischen Akademie der Wissenschaft (Philosophisch-historische Klasse)* (Munich, 1934); A. Dempf,

concept) of "politics" has been important, although it had hardly been discussed up to that time. Thomas had a philosophical conception of the nature of things: he recognized in the temporal order stability and autonomy for each order.[37] With Thomas there is not only a distinction of two functions (this had always been done) but of two defined domains. Nonetheless, the finality of what is human remains unique and is supernatural. There is not only a distinction of powers but a subordination of the *regnum* and *sacerdotium* directing salvation. In short, we have here the teaching of the future: that of Pope Leo XIII.

One text from the commentary on the *Sentences* from 1254 is quite amazing. "Both the spiritual and the secular powers are deduced from divine power. And, therefore, the secular power is under the spiritual power to the extent that the spiritual is presumed to come from God: for instance, in those things which pertain to salvation. And so in these areas the spiritual power should be obeyed more than the secular power. In those things pertaining to the public good the secular power is more to be obeyed than the spiritual power as Matthew says (22:21): 'Give to Caesar the things that are Caesar's.' However, the secular and civil powers are joined as in the pope who holds the pinnacle of both powers, disposing of them as someone who is priest and

---

Sacrum Imperium, 381ff; W. Berges, Die Fürstenspiegel des hohen and späten Mittelalters (Stuttgart, 1938) 113ff., 204ff; W. Ullmann, *Principles of Government and Politics in the Middle Ages* (London, 1961) 111-14; I. T. Eschmann, "St. Thomas Aquinas and the Two Powers, " *Medieval Studies* 20 (1958): 177-205.

[37] "That divine right coming from grace does not take away human right that is from reason" (*ST* II-II, 10, 10); "The rule of Caesar preexisted" (*ST* II-II, 10, 10 ad 2; *Compendium theologiae* 106, 6); see O. Schilling, *Die Staats-und Soziallehre des Thomas von Aquinas* (Munich, 1930).

king."[38] There is no trace of theocracy (as Grabmann pointed out). One knows from other theological areas the care with which Aquinas avoided theologico-political themes even as so many writers of his age did pursue those kinds of themes. In short, after having posed (in a plan of principles) the dualism of power in the sense of a Huguccio, he Dominican listed certain historical and providential facts touching the cases where the two authorities are united in the same person. It can be a case of the temporal domain of the Holy See or of different ways of public law in a Christendom subject to the pope in temporal realities (legal decisions, jurisdiction of a ruler, starting a crusade, etc). One remains a little troubled by the fact that the direct students of Aquinas came to hold theocratic positions (Agostino Trionfo, perhaps Friar Reginald of Piperno); however, if those principles bore special fruit with John of Paris, he was not really his student.

Aquinas himself kept a distance from the hierocratic mind-set of an Innocent IV the end of whose pontificate coincides with Aquinas' writings on church and state.

---

[38] We follow the interpretation of Eschmann who was basically following that of Peter Tischleder, *Ursprung und Träger der Staatsgewalt nach der Lehre des hl. Thomas und seiner Schule* (Cologne, 1923); see *ST* II-II, 60, 6, ad 3.

EXPORING THOMAS AQUINAS

Thomas Aquinas, Vatican II, and Contemporary Theology

C.J. Pinto de Oliveira, O.P.

At critical periods in its history the church becomes aware in new ways of the presence of the great witnesses within its tradition. The Spirit renews the church by means of a fresh understanding of the Gospel, and in the light of this eschatological gift the future opens up and is seen as call and promise. The past with the teachings of past great theologians unfolds new interpretations and messages as they respond to the challenges and problems of the present. Vatican II was precisely that kind of expansion. If the Council wanted to include some orientation toward Thomas Aquinas in its basic plan and in its fruitful and dynamic goals (the re reading of Scripture and Tradition), it deliberately refused, however, to ratify any expression that would give even the appearance of setting the Universal Doctor apart. There could be no splendid isolation, no canonization of his doctrine as a closed system.

Vatican II and the post conciliar church have certainly been sensitive to a climate of suspicion toward all systems of thought. A page in the history of Thomism seems to have been turned, and the present time has gone beyond philosophical and theological systematizations. A "return to St. Thomas" undertaken in the pontificate of Pius IX inaugurated the development which the encyclical *Aeterni Patris* of Leo XIII celebrated in 1879. Now, however, Vatican II inspired a new form of relevancy, one that opens up the theology of Thomas Aquinas. His theology appears as a challenge, as a promise of unprecedented hope in conversation with contemporary thought in the perspective of an ecumenical and structural dialogue. This article will pursue the following themes:

I. The Vicissitudes of Thomism and the Presence of Thomas Aquinas in the Directions of the Second Vatican Council;
II. Questions and Issues Coming from Major Currents of Contemporary Theology;
III. Recent Theological Directions and Thomas Aquinas.

I. The Vicissitudes of Thomism and the Presence of Thomas Aquinas and the Directions of the Second Vatican Council

Two questions, separate but equally important, should be raised at first. What use did the Council make of Aquinas' teaching? What position did it take concerning the place his teaching was to occupy henceforth in ecclesiastical teaching?

A. Thomism before the Council and Thomas Aquinas' Thought at the Council

A comparison of Vatican II with the two previous Councils—Trent and Vatican I—is instructive. While announcing their intention to remain above the quarrels and details of theological schools, the Fathers of the Council of Trent borrowed from the *Summa theologiae* of Thomas essential and fundamental ideas for their entire dogmatic enterprise.[1] The doctrine of sanctifying grace underlying the decree on justification is a summary of Thomistic teaching brought up to date. This, in turn, is present in the text of the decree where the

---

[1] A. Walz pointed this out in his study "La giustificazione tridentina. Note sul debattito a sul decreto conciliare," *Angelicum* 28 (1951): 97 138; on the place of St. Thomas' doctrine on justification in the conciliar decree, see 134-39.

Council's sacramental and ecclesiological positions are collected. More cautiously but no less effectively, Aquinas supplied Vatican I with some ideas on faith and revelation and on the relationships of both to human reason. His theology influences the theological foundations of the dogmatic constitution *Dei Filius* which was intended to offer the starting point and the basis for the whole conciliar work but which was never finished.[2]

At first, Vatican II seems notable for a sharp break in any continuity with Vatican I. The preparatory schemata distributed to the bishops at the beginning of the Council followed, for the most part, the directions inspiring Vatican I. In their content, references, and style those documents hold characteristics of an academic Thomism even as they pay no attention to problems of contemporary culture and church. The real start of the Council is the decisive positions taken in the fall of 1962; they coincided with the rejection (at least tacit) of prior projects prepared at some length (and cost) as well as with the setting aside of the neo-scholastic theology which they contained and whose lack of credibility they only furthered.[3] Vatican II could not find the new

---

[2] The conciliar text (ch. 2) itself refers to the *Summa theologiae* (*ST*) I, 1. What seems to be important is the general perspective. Basic ideas and distinctions dominating the composition of Dei Filius arise from the problematic of faith and reason, and creation and revelation. They revive and emphasize in the framework of the anti-rationalist polemics of the nineteenth-century neo-Thomistic motifs as the neo-scholastic renewal systematized them (see G. Paradis, "Foi et Raison au Premier Concile du Vatican," in *De doctrina Concilii Vatican Primi* [Rome, 1969] 221 281).

[3] The projects emanating from the Conciliar Commission "*De doctrina fidei et morum*" (with Cardinal Ottaviani presiding) were concerned with a precise, often rigid formulation of traditional doctrine. Thanks to the publication of the *Acta Synodalia Sacrosancti Concilii Oecumenici Vaticani II* (Vatican City, 1967) we can compare the neo-scholastic purport of the primitive schemata with the definitive wording adopted by the Council. The judgment expressed in the following pages is the

orientations needed by the church in that established theology then enjoying public respect; it could not assist in fashioning true conciliar texts.

The constitutions, declarations, and decrees emanating from the Council are the work of compromise and are considered to be pastoral. A coherence given by a technical language or a systematic homogeneity is not central in them. The key ideas of revelation, church, priesthood, mission, union of Christians, presence of the Spirit in the church and history, the idea of liberty are present in an empirical, descriptive way. Most often they develop theological intuitions coming out of several currents of renewal. Because his doctrine remains a point of reference (if not the first source of inspiration) for great theologians such as M.-D Chenu, Yves Congar, Edward Schillebeeckx, and Karl Rahner, Aquinas is present without being named. A study of the interventions of those attending the Council permits us to evaluate the strength of a theological approach whose fidelity to Aquinas is on the same level as its opening to contemporary social and individual problematics. We can mention here the example of Cardinal Karol Wojtyla's insistence on the pivotal ideas of liberty, creation, and salvation, their relationship to each other, and the importance of the redemption to clarify both Christian existence and the sense of history in the Council's *Gaudium et Spes* and *Dignitas Humanae Personae*.[4] While the Council rejected a Thomism fixed in abstract formulas and so went beyond fossilized theological systems, it showed impressively an intense and creative fidelity to the doctrine and spirit of

---

result of such comparisons in terms of *Lumen Gentium*, *Dei Verbum*, and *Gaudium et Spes*.

[4] Cf. C. J. Pinto de Oliveira, "Gospel and Rights of Man. The Theological Originality of John Paul II," in *John Paul II and the Rights of Man* (Fribourg, 1980).

Aquinas. There is nothing surprising in that. Vatican II was the outcome of a vast process of ecclesial growth where the presence of theology became more inventive as it associated a predilection for Aquinas with bold innovations. When the modernist crisis was at its height producing troubling relations between church, scripture and tradition, J. M. Lagrange drew from Aquinas a realistic, clear and operational understanding of history and human freedom under divine action; he also succeeded in legitimizing the use of a historical method and of critical procedures in the service of a tradition of real exegesis. The way was open for the contemporary biblical renewal which the encyclical *Divino Afflante Spiritu* of Pius XII in 1943 affirmed at the right moment and which the dogmatic constitution *Dei Verbum* would take up again more extensively in 1965. Was it not an inventive and dynamic fidelity to Aquinas that served L. J. Lebret as a source of human economics and as an inspiration for an integral development of persons and peoples? That was affirmed by *Gaudium et Spes* and the encyclical *Populorum Progressio* as an urgent requirement for the future if not for the very survival of humanity?

Vatican II showed an openness and selective discernment toward Aquinas that it adopted vis a vis other thinkers within the living tradition in the church. That discernment prompted it to abandon all systems, systems sometimes so frozen that tradition and system took on a polemical and defensive bias. Vatican II linked the church of the present day and its future to biblical, patristic, liturgical, and theological sources. Forgoing the earlier, well-worn paths of the Counter Reformation, it expressed confidence in the spontaneous spirit of original principles and charisms in the great theologians waiting to be rediscovered.

The synthesis of Aquinas, courageously and clearly stripped of academic rigidity, profits by being read and expanded in the light of post conciliar renewal and in the perspectives opened by today's church.

B. The Doctrine of Aquinas and the Basic Directions of the Council

We can consider what is fundamental, essential, and productive in Aquinas by citing four dynamics fashioning the main stages of the renewal begun by the Council. They point out places and conditions for a fruitful encounter between conciliar orientations and implications, and the theology of Aquinas.

1. Perhaps the broadest and most understandable theological position at work in the Council is the harmonious integration of creation in the work of redemption. Its counterpart lies in the understanding of history as the dynamic field of salvation arranged and subordinated to an eschatological fulfillment. From this it follows that the whole world and all of history are conceived as a process of liberation and as an achievement of the Paschal Mystery which the bestowed Holy Spirit realizes in the church and in the world. Such a vision of salvation—integrating, unifying, and energizing history as it becomes a source of grace and responsibility for all—is present everywhere in Vatican II, especially in the most innovative texts of the Council. Chapters from the first part of the constitution *Gaudium et Spes* develop those themes.

2. *Gaudium et Spes* sets forth in particular the mission of the Spirit to explain these motifs and their origins. It is a universal mission yet one

which is varied in its results. "The Spirit operates in history":[5] it brings to success God's work of salvation and inspires, strengthens, and rectifies the aspirations, demands, and movements of human progress. An affirmation of the Holy Spirit in various activities and effects explains the unifying yet pluralistic vision that the Council proposes within history, one tending towards a definitive, eschatological fulfillment. This explains too why Vatican II fully acknowledges the validity of the temporal, physical, economic, and cultural orders. The Spirit acts in a certain way in the People of God; it guarantees the specific mission and the indefectibility of the church as source of truth and salvation. Since the church is from the Spirit, it is called to pay homage to values and truths appearing in a partial or less important way in the life and aspirations of people. The same Spirit appears in religions and in a secularized world: it is a principle of all truth and of all good. The presence of the Spirit is thus the first principle of the life of the church, of Christian existence and discernment.

3. The church is presented in a doctrinally logical (although semantically new) definition as the sacrament of salvation and of the reconciliation of the whole of humanity. This expands the idea of sacrament beyond the realm of ritual. Above all, this understanding of church as the fundamental sacrament characterizes the community of salvation as a reality sent, as a

---

[5] Cf. the author's "'L'Esprit agit dans l'histoire.' La totalisation hégélienne de l'histoire confrontée avec les perspectives du Concile Vatican II," *Hegel et la théologie contemporaine* (Neuchâtel, 1977) 54, 73.

mission, as a search for a unity and as a place. The church is the eschatological gift of unity and peace; this unity has been begun but is badly in need of the full union of believers, of all religious people, indeed of all men and women injured by atheism, idolatry, and paganism.

4. Finally, a fourth point. Faith described in the constitution *Dei Verbum* underlies the fundamental positions of the Council. Faith is characterized first as the conversion of the whole person to God, to the Living God revealing himself through Christ in history and existing now through the grace of the Spirit. Believing emerges as a personal encounter which the church raises up and encourages; faith collaborates with the intellectual adherence which men and women give freely to the grace of the Spirit. The union of grace with intelligence and liberty inevitably leads to an insistence on the fact that the action of the Spirit engenders a search for and an adherence to the truth as well as to an awakening and the process of liberty. Here we have an inner perspective and dynamic: it marks the openness of Vatican II and fashioning its particular originality. People can search for and find truth only in complete liberty. The Spirit of holiness and love makes the church a source of truth and a guardian of liberty. A pneumatological and anthropological spirituality complements the objective, historical, and communal aspects that the Council accentuated. This initiates a stronger missiological and ecumenical opening in the church as well as comprehensive and dynamic

positions with regard to politics, economics and culture.

Having noted these basic points, let us underline the mutual benefit that resulted from the encounter of the conciliar message with a renewed understanding of the theology of Thomas Aquinas. The conciliar message could not and did not express itself in a homogeneous and rigid ideology. Particularly with Aquinas' theology the conciliar renewal and the post conciliar challenges offer unprecedented opportunities for a new vitality and fecundity. First, Aquinas' theology itself returns to its basic principles when it encounters the fundamental aspects that the Council raised in viewing the one world of creation and salvation. The Council's insistence on the role of the Holy Spirit in the life of the church, in Christian existence and in the history of peoples, cultures, religions, is an insistence on the Spirit as the source of truth and liberty (with truth emphasized as much as liberty in the preparation and progress of faith). These conciliar contributions are welcome and beneficial to the work of theological renewal. They help to rectify and restore balance to some Thomistic systems whose elaboration in historical and cultural forms had hardened into partial formulas and polemics. Furthermore, Aquinas' synthesis itself is marked by certain constraints coming from its *ordo disciplinae*, that is to say, from the method and model which scholastic theology used. As to the content, that same medieval context led Aquinas to treat certain basic questions of faith rather unsatisfactorily. His teaching did not close the doors on the emergence of a theology of the Inquisition even as it left open the way to a theology of religious liberty, ecumenism, and wider salvation.[6]

---

[6] On non-belief see *ST* II-II, 10 & 11. In *ST* II-II, 11, 3, the doctrine of tolerance is formulated in the objections, supported by authorities

By encountering and absorbing the message of Vatican II the basic principles of the *Summa theologiae* were thrown into a new relief. The mission of the Spirit, the new law of the Gospel, liberty at the heart of faith, eschatology anticipated on earth, the virtues of faith and hope, and the primacy of charity as "form of the virtues"[7] were aspects which previously Thomism had not been able to employ. They became productive, however, in that springtime initiated by the Council for the church and the world.

C. Thomas Aquinas: The Commendation of the Council

The general directions of the Council and its attitude (both comprehensive and selective) toward different strains of Catholic tradition pointed out the limits and the contexts of life and teaching that could use Aquinas. The recommendation of Aquinas was the result of debate and mature reflection set amid a series of discussions and arguments over a decree on the formation of priests. That schema distributed to the conciliar fathers in May, 1963, was the revised version of a document elaborated by the preparatory commission; it revived the prescriptions of the old Code of Canon Law (1366, 2) stipulating that the "perennial philosophy" should be taught to future priests

---

drawn from Scripture and from Greek thought. The article's teaching also draws inspiration from the anti-Donatist writings of St. Augustine.

[7] Pertinent here are basic texts of the *Summa theologiae*. On the doctrine of the mission of the Spirit, see *ST* I, 43, a pivotal question situated between a contemplation of the Trinity in itself and a look at the plan and the works of creation and salvation. This question should be brought into dialogue with three areas: the treatise on the New Law (the evangelical Law which is the Law of liberty and of the Spirit [*ST* I-II, 106 108]), liberty at the heart of faith (*ST* II-II, 4 and *De Veritate*, 14, 2), and charity as the "form of the virtues" (*ST* II-II, 23, 8). These themes of Aquinas' teaching fashion an original theology faithful to the Gospel and tradition; they are able today to orient the life of a Christian and of the church.

"according to the plan, teaching, and principles of St. Thomas."[8] Formation in theology should develop "with St. Thomas as the teacher of philosophy." Those texts often received praise,[9] although more and more interventions asked for a flexible statement, one attentive to engaging in dialogue with different cultures and to recognize the important contributions of modern and contemporary philosophies. Requests coming from representatives of Oriental churches were especially insistent. Balancing the different opinions,[10] the Council was able to reach unanimity on the following points:

1. Philosophical formation, mentioned first, does not refer explicitly to Aquinas: "The philosophical disciplines will be taught," says the decree *Optatam Totius*, "in a way which will lead seminarians from the very beginning to a solid and coherent knowledge of the human person, the world, and God. To succeed in this, they will rely on "the philosophical patrimony which is forever valid."[11] "It is supremely efficacious for assuring the fundamentals of the faith and for gathering usefully and without danger the fruits of a healthy progress." The

---

[8] Cf. *Acta Synodalia*..., vol. III, Period III, par. VII, 523 524.
[9] An Australian bishop declared of Aquinas: "He is to be praised in the highest way and totally retained" (*Acta Synodalia*, 969).
[10] Recommending Thomas Aquinas amid cultural diversities, the needs of ecumenical dialogue, and the theologies of Oriental Churches are the interventions of Msgr. Hoffner (*Acta Synodalia*, 860), the Patriarch of the Melkites (Ibid., 900) and the Patriarch of the Maronites (Ibid., 938). The views of the conferences of bishops in India (Ibid., 895 896), in Indonesia (Ibid., 970), and in Canada (Ibid., 951) were important.
[11] *Optatam totius*, 415. A note refers to the encyclical *Humani Generis*, citing the exact pages of the *Acta Apostolicae Sedis* (42 [1950]: 571, 575) where Pius XII detailed the content of this "philosophical patrimony forever valid" and justified the attachment of the church to the "Angelic Doctor" by virtue of the "eminent superiority of his method," and of "the harmony of his doctrine with divine revelation."

Council continued: "Attention must also be paid to more recent fields of philosophical research, especially to what exercises a significant influence in a particular country, and also to recent scientific progress. . ." Here the decree touches on ideas from the encyclical *Ecclesiam Suam* where Paul VI in August, 1964, insisted upon the necessity and format of dialogue.

2. Conciliar orientations in the teaching of dogmatic theology refer explicitly to Aquinas. After having assigned to biblical, patristic and historical sources a primordial place, the same conciliar decree adds: "In terms of the mysteries of salvation, seminarians should learn to penetrate them more deeply and to perceive their logic through reflection, with St. Thomas as teacher" (*Optatam totius* # 16). A note here refers to the discourses of Pius XII and Paul VI which emphasize how Aquinas' doctrine "guides and stimulates research." Addresses by Paul VI in 1964 and 1965 had helped to clear the way for those conciliar decisions by declaring that fidelity to St. Thomas "far from resulting in a system unproductively turned in on itself is capable of successfully applying its principles, method, and spirit to new tasks that the problematic of our day proposes for the consideration of Christian thinkers."[12] The Declaration *Gravissimum Educationis* on Christian education, citing that same speech of Paul VI, proposes to Catholic faculties and

---

[12] Allocution of Paul VI at the Sixth International Thomist Convention, Sept. 10, 1965. *Optatam totius* refers to that conference (note 36 of the conciliar decree) without giving any reference. It is also cited by *Gravissimum educationis*.

universities a program of courage and freedom in research: "New problems and areas of research created by progress in the modern world will be carefully studied. It will be possible to grasp more clearly how faith and reason unite to attain to truth." The conciliar declaration continues: "Doing that, one need only follow the way opened by the Doctors of the Church and especially by St. Thomas" (# 10). To connect Aquinas' doctrine with all of tradition as a rallying point and not as a rupture and to extol his method and his spirit as an incitement to research and dialogue in the church with different forms of culture this is the essence of papal directives in agreement with the orientation and practice of the Council.

II. Questions and Issues Coming from Major Currents of Contemporary Theology

Furthered by the climate of liberty and research created and encouraged by Vatican II, Catholic theology is seeking to profit by the orientations of the Council. It has also revived the approach of viewing in a more or less critical fashion an ensemble of cultural, social, and even political influences. What are some characteristic features of prominent, current theologies? What are the assumptions, methods and fields of research or thought which they explore? This is a critique of Thomistic systems even as it contributes to a renewed and creative understanding of the theology of Aquinas.

A. Positive or Critical Assumptions

Contemporary theology has set clear goals, and its ambition is daringly universal. It seems to bypass seminaries and ecclesiastical institutions and to dispense with models and systems of the past. It faces problems created by culture, indeed considers them to be a starting point for all research. It uses scientific discoveries and speaks the language they employ and generally engages the methods accepted by the scholarly world if not by the experts.

The following are characteristics of a theology that wants to be present and active in today's society. Communication is ecumenical, going beyond the limits of systems, especially of neo-scholastic systems. Conversely, a philosophy of the subject, a critical philosophy, a philosophy of history, a philosophy of science, and a hermeneutical method universally applicable to Scripture, to tradition and to statements by the magisterium of the church attracts theologians. There are different ways of expressing experience or of analyzing existence in our personal life and in society. These are the starting points (either stated or implicit) for dynamic currents in Christian theology in the West.

B. A Triple Challenge: Theologies of Existence, History, and Liberation

Let us illustrate what is taking place by looking briefly at three representative theologies, those of existence, history, and liberation.

1. Theologies of existence come from the union of three factors whose persistence guarantees their influence. Here faith is described as a decision involving a person in authentic existence before the light and by virtue of the Gospel message. Second, the Gospel message is grasped and interpreted by a hermeneutic analyzing the meaning of life existentially, taking into consideration the mythical representations of the New Testament at their symbolic value, and relativizing ecclesiastical formulas considered in their doctrinal ("notional") content. An understanding of

salvation, revelation, and faith come from a philosophy of the person and leaves little space for objective knowledge of God and salvation. Here a person pursues two kinds of knowledge: the first brings a liberating understanding of existence, subjects, self, and others; the second gives an objectifying knowledge which can grasp, measure and manipulate objects, a knowledge which would be servile and subjugating if applied to subjects (humans) and would become idolatrous if it aspired to encircle God, to reduce God to the condition of an object, to dispose of God like a thing.

No one should underestimate the importance of existential theologies whose pioneer was Rudolf Bultmann. They emerge where Christians try to speak of divine transcendence. Their strength comes from the fact that they gather culture and Christian thought into a coherent doctrine. The idea of a "faith decision" confers a cultural vitality on the doctrine of fiducial faith, something quite basic for the piety and theology of the church of the Reformation. Existential theologies were inspired by the early elaborations of Martin Heidegger who influenced contemporary thought extensively by his efforts to reinterpret the history of Western thinking by examining closely the ways of being and the depths of language. There is too a prolongation of Kantianism that here rejects for theoretical reasoning any capacity to know God.

2. Theologies of history from their beginning have clearly shown a break with traditional doctrinal elaborations. They hold the Hellenization of

Christianity to be a fact already achieved before the patristic era and strengthened during the Middle Ages. Theology must begin anew: it should refuse the framework and forms of Greek thought, especially its cyclic conception of history. The history of salvation, understood as a series of biblical events—centered in the Christological reality and aspiring to eschatological fulfillment—is both the means and object of revelation. The entire field of theology would be only a hermeneutics—itself historical—of the history of salvation. Some dispute the postulation of biblical history as the only expression of revelation. Consequently, a dogmatic enterprise pursued by the church especially in the history of Councils is held in low esteem.

Understood fully and intelligently, the history of salvation does fashion the thought-form of divine revelation (as the opening of *Dei Verbum* points out), and this fact still underlies Christian theology. Theological articulation remains to be done, so that the history of salvation can become real in the heart of human existence. This history should reach out to the history of humanity and to the resources and challenges of cultures.

3. Theologians use similar theological expressions today as they emphasize the reality of the history of salvation and find in it an inspiration for the Christian life. The history of salvation leads to eschatology present now and efficacious in a promise generating hope. This theological current (for instance, Jürgen Moltmann) stresses the fundamental, biblical

fact that the divine revealing word is promise. Revelation is not to be perceived as an "epiphany," a disclosing of God's being. Revelation speaks of God as coming; the action of God enables the action of human beings. Ahead are new possibilities of that action creative in time and in freedom. Hope makes present things to come even as it urges Christian action forward. Promise creates something quite new in history, producing unprecedented events and possibilities. Through God's promise and our hope, history is in the process of becoming. Strictly speaking, a theology that is truly submissive to the divine word must be defined as "Hope seeking understanding." This would correct the traditional claims of connecting theological comprehension only to a knowledge of the faith ("Faith seeking understanding"). The theology of hope follows upon theologies of history (as with Wolfhart Pannenberg). There is a refusal to have only a God revealed and recognized in his being, while possibilities of knowledge arising from an understanding of faith are denied or marginalized. Only knowledge that is consubstantial with dynamic hope creating action and fashioning history will serve as a primal and inventive principle for theology and for the life of the Christian and of the church.

Eschatology—school manuals had relegated it to an appendix called the "Last Things"—is again becoming a source, even a first principle of theology. This renewal is the source of theologies of liberation. The structure and legitimacy of theological knowledge shows an underlying affinity between the theologies of hope and the theologies of liberation. For both the divine Word is essentially, primordially liberating. Witnessed through scripture and the tradition of the church, the living Word origin, truth, salvation exists in the act of liberating, in the process or praxis which constitutes the people of the New Covenant. Theologies of liberation are fashioned by liberty, justice, knowledge – and, even more, by the recognition of God as liberator. It is not enough to say that the message of salvation is human improvement or that a liberation in the temporal or political order would be a corollary close to a conversion of the heart. More radical than so called political theologies (developed in Germany after the war) the theologies of liberation first refuse dichotomies: spiritual versus temporal or personal versus social. These arise out of the privatization of the understanding of salvation, a privatization giving preference to personal salvation, to the pardon of personal sins, and to the sanctification of souls. The new starting point is to go beyond accurate but abstract distinctions. The complete liberation of the human person and the knowledge of God must be grasped firmly as an indivisible totality. God's manifestation, the revelation of God in history, takes place in times and places where the oppressed are being liberated and where they are liberating the oppressors.

If we describe praxis as an activity of liberation, cultural and global, social and personal, we could say of theology that it is "Praxis seeking understanding." Praxis is the reflection of the church on living and committed faith.

III. Recent Theological Directions and Thomas Aquinas

Those projects of current theologies just mentioned seem removed from Aquinas. More by silence or omission, his doctrine after the Council was often the object of reservation or suspicion. The climate of suspicion can be explained by a whole range of criticisms accumulated through the centuries, and Catholic theology was inclined to take them seriously. These criticisms could be drawn together in the censure found in Heideggerian thought and shared by some Christian thinkers: the authentic synthesis of Thomas Aquinas is a model of ontotheology, of a theology in bondage to metaphysics, of a theology which might have overlooked the originality and the transcendence of the God revealed by Jesus Christ. Is it surprising that Thomistic theology would be labeled as incapable of grasping and legitimizing the important data of the Christian message and the urgent demands of today's thought? Isn't Thomism the opposite of the theologies of existence, of history and of liberation?

A. Thomas Aquinas and the Crisis of Foundational Theology

This question leads us into the deepest and most radical of contemporary interrogations. We touch here the crisis which is affecting the foundations of theology. This universal and basic examination is exciting and risky. From the Middle Ages on, we meet as *quaestiones disputatae* issues like the existence of God, and we encounter treatises on divine mysteries in theological *summae*. Today, however, there is a methodical doubt, a questioning of the fundamentals of the faith born of the insecurity of many believers. At the same time, these theologies ponder the real origins and originality of the Christian fact; they ask about God revealed in Jesus Christ, the person of Jesus, salvation in the Gospel. They inquire into the universality of the Church's mission, the necessity of dialogue, the collective understanding of human problems including the very survival of humanity. These questions have an impact on the faith of the Christian people and public opinion. Theology must preserve the transcendence of the evangelical message and at the same time increase the stability of the political, economic, cultural order along with the autonomy of scientific knowledge and research. Equally strong is the imperative to ground the liberating and originating action of human rights and of peace in the world in the primordial exigency of the Christian ethic.

If we look closely at contemporary theologies and their critiques, we notice an ensemble of paradoxes. Showing the lordship of God (through Christ and in the Spirit) acting universally on the world, history, and existence – this seems to be the concern of a theology intending to be faithful to the Gospel message. Doesn't any attachment of the world to God imply God's dependence on the universe whose demiurge or ultimate legitimation he would become? Aren't ethical inferences binding God to the moral order or events localizing him in history to be stigmatized as ethically or historically simplistic? Regardless, a consensus seems to exist in contemporary theological projects that any metaphysical way of having access to God or of articulating the data of revelation should be set aside. To sum up, the Heideggerian critique of ontotheology means to qualify and even reject any route going from Being to God, any view resulting in the identification of God with a Supreme Being. This approach would destroy God: it is the elder sibling if not the parent of atheism. It brings God down to the level of beings where God would be only the first in a series or first in an order supposedly univocal.

So Thomas Aquinas could receive a dual reproof: one of being a theologian of an abstract cosmos, and one of offering an ontotheology. "Even the greatest representatives such as Thomas Aquinas escapes with difficulty the Heideggerian critique of metaphysics," declared Claude Geffré. The French Dominican looks for a "non metaphysical theology" whose task will consist in "going beyond theological objectivism and theological subjectivism."[13]

B. A True Fundamental Theology

Let us now turn to the synthesis of Thomas Aquinas in its original dynamic. What are its theological foundations? What positive contributions can it make to contemporary theology?

1. *Aquinas' Originality.* The central originality of Aquinas—it has lasted up to now—springs from the breadth and depth of his preliminary design. For him, theology is *sacra doctrina*: knowledge of God himself and in himself, knowledge whose subject is God revealed. The starting point is not philosophical, for Aquinas has in view theological knowledge. The primal object of this knowing becomes the light for the whole range of mysteries and realities which flow from God. Theological knowledge becomes possible by virtue of the transcending expansion of the intellect; while staying in its proper domain of rational capacity, theology receives from faith—further, from the theological triad of faith hope charity—a deep potentiality for the intellect. The constitutive moment of theological understanding and belief is an orientation and subordination of creation to salvation, of history to eschatological fulfillment, of human existence to holiness in the Spirit, of the ethical order to theological life.

---

[13] See "Théologie" in *Encyclopedia Universalis* 15 (Paris, 1973) 1090.

We can emphasize, in spite of the diversity of thought forms, the fundamental agreement of the major orientations of Vatican II with the fundamental principles of the teaching of Aquinas. Theology must have recourse to creation interpreted in an ontological register, in the light of Being as well as in the mediation of history. By studying the network of conditions of existence there can emerge an integral Christian plan of personal, social, and political ethics. And yet, these mediations—ontological, historical, existential, ethical, political—flow back to the God of revelation received in faith; their stability, their capacity to be known and illuminated flow from this source in which they can participate. From that same source, they receive a coherence within a theological system; they arrange themselves in essentially different degrees while being united in an analogical way.

Contemporary issues lead us to consider more closely and to bring out more explicitly aspects of a theological understanding to which earlier Thomists paid little attention and which Aquinas himself never emphasized. In a single movement, theological understanding, supported by faith, recognizes the transcendence of the revealed God who is its object: it also recognizes the consistency of reason and of the metaphysical work which it can develop in history and in the ethical order. The calling of the human race is at the heart of the divine plan of the creator and savior. Theology develops out of a desire—to paraphrase and condense Aquinas[14]—for knowledge: a knowledge of God,

---

[14] See *ST* II-II, 2, 10; *In librum Boethii de Trinitate expositio*, q. 2.

a knowledge with God as the object. Theology transcends, attracts, and elevates the one who knows. Theology has roots in faith precisely as it is intellectual; knowledge ushers in a theological life. Theology has too an eschatological tension of hope and the transforming force of charity intent on widening and deepening.

2. *Theological Knowledge and Existential Decision.* Let us compare further some of Aquinas' positions with problematics and contributions of contemporary theology. Existential theologies have insisted rightly on the importance and influence of decisions in the birth and development of faith. Decision gives an orientation to Christian existence and so decision will have a major role in theological understanding. Avoiding every concordism and respecting differences between problematic and noetic horizons, one can find in the content and language proper to Aquinas aspects similar to existential theologies: an elevation of the will and a primacy of spiritual affectivity are at the root of the act of faith. At the beginning of faith there is a love of truth, an absolute love of the only truth. The desire to know the true God is awakened and sustained by the divine message resounding in the human person who in turn is looking for fulfillment and destiny. One can never insist enough on the intimate presence of faith and hope at the heart of faith. Aquinas developed in his theology a synergy of intellect and desire as first principles of knowledge with teleological and eschatological perspectives. The originality of this theology appears precisely in the fact that faith rooted in

affectivity and volition moves towards freedom even as it remains essentially and primordially an activity of knowledge. Appearing in the interiority of knowing powers, faith asks of people that they pass beyond their limits. This approach pays homage to the First Truth, creative and saving. Theology recognizes the infinite character of divine Truth and the finite character of the created intellect.

"The perception of truth tends towards ultimate truth." Theology tends toward Truth without seeking to monopolize it. Theology should refuse to enclose divine transcendence in notional limits or to make equal all the kinds of judgments required by progress in human knowledge. Theology learns from faith that human knowledge is being called to go beyond itself, to live in the "non-objectivizing" realm. Desire for objectivity should yield to the demands of faith's subject matter: divine mystery. The intellect affirms divine mystery by denying limitations to human conceptual representations and by deconstructing its rational procedure. Such is the properly theological origin of analogy which Aquinas developed systematically by borrowing certain philosophical elements from the gnoseology and logic of Aristotle. The *analogia entis* does not take the place of the *analogia fidei* with which it conforms to a certain degree, and which it must serve by spreading out and adapting itself to theological requirements. Following Aquinas, we can only agree with Karl Barth's legitimate irritation at an *analogia entis* making God one being among others, even the head of all beings. Likewise, we can welcome Bultmannian and post Bultmannian perspectives which refuse to enclose God and the work of salvation inside the limits of an objectivizing knowledge. For Aquinas, however, the theological project remains a work of the intellect, an intellect enriched by transcendence validated by divine creation and actualized by revealing Word and faith.

3. *St. Thomas and Ontotheology.* Stripped of their technical presentation and uprooted from a carefully shaped system of thought, Heidegger's critiques and insights have tended to become, if not the common stance, at least an obligatory point of reference for a good number of contemporary theologians. Through a genealogical reconstruction influenced by Nietzsche, Heidegger proposed to uncover and expose the basic orientations inspiring Western thought. From its beginnings and empowered by Plato the metaphysics of Greek philosophy has missed the question of Being by overlooking its difference from individual beings. Metaphysics searched for a basis for contingent beings, searched for a ground to explain them: the existence of an uncaused cause. This ends in postulating the existence of a Supreme Being who is presented as an infinite being. It will found and legitimize the universe of beings, the totality of finite beings. Heidegger did not exceed the limits of his own territory, the history and hermeneutics of philosophical thought. Applications of his philosophy, however, soon attracted the attention of theologians. For them, the misfortune of Christian theology consisted precisely in its sanction of Greek metaphysics,

and this caused its greatest error: to misunderstand the specificity of the Christian message and to substitute for the revealed God the Supreme Being of ontotheology.

We must be grateful to critics who denounce such theological deviations as dangerous temptations precisely because they are subtle ones. Such warnings can be salutary if they incite us to a more attentive reading and to a deeper hermeneutical understanding of tradition, especially of the major positions of Aquinas. In the service of theological elaboration, he employed anthropology as well as ontology, a cosmology and an ethics drawn in substance and form from Greek and Roman thinkers. He did this deliberately. Replying to his critics, he declared with a touch of irony that by using philosophical doctrines in the service of theological understanding, far from diluting the wine of divine wisdom, the Christian teacher was changing water into wine.

His synthesis, the *Summa Theologiae*, organizes the elements of *sacra doctrina* in their splendor from a strictly epistemological viewpoint and yet retains the clear characteristics of a theology tending toward the transcendence of divine mysteries. He never tired of probing Scripture according to the methods and resources at his disposal. He inquired into the meaning and coherence of the revealing Word and work of God. In anything touching the systematic work of theology, Aquinas mobilized all the resources of reason and culture so as to obtain for the believer and for the church an intellectual penetration, rationally articulated, of the mystery of God. God appears in the life of the Trinity and in a generous creative and saving love. Aquinas' intention to reveal as much as possible the mystery of God through the "full enterprise of reason" needs inspiration and genius in finding a theological synthesis. The *ordo disciplinae*, the rigor of the method adopted by Aquinas, leading to the unity of God before the Trinity of Persons, proceeds from the human person with its capabilities and limitations to the understanding of human relations with God. Only then does he turn to the study of Christology, soteriology, and eschatology.

At the beginning of the *Summa theologiae* we meet the theme of the ability of the human person to reach God. Aquinas stressed the value and the means of a rational approach to God, as well as the possibilities, limits, and conditions of theological language. Aquinas did give a quasi-definition of God: the One Who Is, Subsistent Being, associating the experience of reason to the audacious version that the Greek Bible gave to the liberating theophany "I Am the One Who Is." Aquinas approached the study of the divine Trinity only after the unity of God is identified as the Subsistent Being, First and Perfect, whose existence could be rationally established.

A perfect being, however, is a stumbling block for contemporary thinkers who see there the result of an ontotheology. Does not this system deduce the mystery of the Trinity from a metaphysically constructed theism? Doesn't it reduce Christian theology to a natural, rationally based theology? The theology of Thomas Aquinas is different: it wants to show that a natural and rational knowledge of God is possible and accessible to any human intellect. Such knowledge need not lead to the subtle fabrication of an intellectual idol. It leads to a knowledge that is true but imperfect, insufficient for salvation, a partial knowledge. When the coming of the Divine Word is announced it does not invite the human person to stay in a closed world but to open itself up to the transcendence and the magnanimity of revelation. Revelation subsumes and surpasses every possible form of knowledge of God. Knowledge obtained by faith—theology is its rationally articulated elaboration—will integrate in intellectual and existential coherence the knowledge of a God whose validity and boundaries it values. Enlightened by faith, theological understanding grasps the mystery of the Unity and Trinity of God, and today theologians find approaches to systematic reflection which start from the Trinity's life. To contemplate the Trinity, Aquinas thought it necessary to begin with all that reason and faith can know about God: the transcendence of the divine Being and the divine activity whose goal is creation. Aquinas then looks at life—thought, will, and love—in the human person, the image of God. Men and women by means of participation and analogy can have some knowledge of the One who is the Principle of human beings and the Goal of human destinies. Theology distinguishes, analyzes, and arranges potential and diversely real modalities of knowledge in order to approach the divine mystery. It respects God's transcendence, and at the same time it respects the human being's dignity and weakness. Contemporary theologians may prefer other approaches but they must confront the teaching of Aquinas correctly understood.

Aquinas' Spirituality for Christ's Faithful Living in the World
Walter Principe, C. S. B.

The following pages attempt to explore some of the ways that Thomas Aquinas' theology can contribute to the spirituality of people living and ministering in secular society or in the world.[1] The term *world* or *worldly* has had a considerable history in Christian thought and spirituality. The Johannine gospel and the first letter of John frequently rail against the world and the worldly. On the other hand, the same gospel has this striking text: "Yes, for God so loved the world as to give the only-Begotten Son, that whoever believes in him may not die but may have eternal life. God did not send the Son into the world to condemn the world but that the world might be saved through him" (3:16-17). In the Middle Ages, the theme of contempt for the world (*contemptus mundi*) was frequently developed, especially among monastic authors. Until quite recently it affected Christian spirituality, often producing in Christ's faithful living and working in the world an unhealthy tension between their spiritual life, their life of Christian prayer and worship, and their family life, their work life, and their life of leisure and recreation. Catholic Action movements earlier in this century were an attempt by workers, students, and family members to bring the Gospel into their daily lives and to help reshape the institutions they worked and lived in and the attitudes of the people they met there. This and

---

[1] The terms "Christ's faithful lay people" or "Christ's faithful," used by John Paul II in his encyclical *Christifideles laici* after the synod on the laity, are preferable, despite their clumsiness, to the simpler term *laity*, whose connotation is negative since it is usually defined as "those who are not clerics."

other movements—among which was the influence of Thomas Aquinas' thought through some of his enlightened disciples—led to the dramatically new outlook of the document of by Vatican II on the Church in the world of today, *Gaudium et Spes*.

Some Historical Background

"Spirituality" is used often today to speak about the doctrine or tradition of some acknowledged leader or example of a spirituality, e.g., the spirituality of St. Paul, St. Francis of Assisi, or St. Benedict. Along the same lines, one speaks of the spirituality of a group, e.g., Dominican spirituality, Jesuit spirituality, priestly or lay spirituality. But this use of spirituality for a doctrine or tradition is on a second and derived level. If there were no primary or original level of spirituality, that is, a really lived spirituality, there would be no doctrine or tradition to pass on, no teaching to examine. This primary or original level, the existential level, is my area of discussion.

Today there are many attempts to define spirituality on this primary level. I define or describe spirituality as "life in the Spirit" (life in the Holy Spirit) but with the immediate addition: "as brothers and sisters of Jesus Christ and as daughters and sons of the Father." This definition can, I think, be derived from chapter eight of Paul's *Letter to the Romans*. The whole chapter deserves a careful, meditative reading. Here are some lines that are significant. "What the Law could not do because of the weakness of human nature, God did, sending his own Son in the same human nature as any sinner to be a sacrifice for sin, and condemning sin in that human nature. This was so that the Law's requirements might be fully satisfied in us as we direct our lives not by our natural inclinations but by the spirit.... Those who are living by their natural inclinations have their minds on the things human nature desires; those who live in the spirit have their minds on spiritual things. And human nature has nothing to look forward to but death, while the spirit looks forward to life and peace, because the outlook of disordered human nature is opposed to God, since it does not submit to God's Law, and indeed it cannot, and those who live by their natural inclinations can never be pleasing to God. You, however, live not by your natural inclinations, but by the spirit, since the Spirit of God has made a home in you. Indeed, anyone who does not have the Spirit of Christ does not belong to him" (Romans 8:3-9). One could go on quoting the whole of this marvelous hymn to God's love for us and God's call for us to live in our spirit by the Holy Spirit.

In the above text, there is a translation problem: the translation of *pneuma* and *sarx* (*spiritus* and *caro* in Latin), terms used by Paul to describe a tension that he sees in Christian life. Some translations speak of "spirit" and "flesh," and others speak of "spirit" (or "spiritual") but translate *sarx* as "natural inclinations" or "disordered human nature." Why omit the more literal translation of *sarx* as "flesh"? Because much harm has been done throughout Christian history by misreading Paul on this point, a point that is important for our concerns with spirituality in a secular society.[2]

For Paul, the spirit in us is the whole human person. This spirit has many aspects, and the whole human person is led, moved, or inspired by the Holy Spirit of God. This includes our bodies, our emotions, our human activity, which is usually bodily and emotional in some way. Everything in us is influenced by the Spirit. On the other hand, *Sarx* or flesh is not our body or the material element in us, but everything in our totality as human

---

[2] The translation of *sarx* as "natural inclinations" is not entirely satisfactory for it gives the impression that nature and the inclinations of nature are of themselves opposed to the Spirit or to God. "Disorderly inclination" would be greatly preferable.

persons that is opposed to the leading, moving, or inspiring activity of the Spirit. Hence the translation should be "natural inclinations" or a better one, "disordered human nature." So for Paul the elements in us closer to matter - our bodies, our emotions or passions, our bodily activities - can be and are spiritual if they share in our total service of God in and by the Holy Spirit. On the other hand, that which is most immaterial in us - our minds, our intellects, our wills - can be flesh or fleshly if they are opposed to the Holy Spirit. In fact, in the *Letter to the Colossians* 2:18 the Pauline text, speaking about some proud teachers who were boasting about visions they claimed to have had, says that they are "puffed up by their *mind of flesh*" (*nous tes sarkos*). Here the text explicitly associates whatever is opposed to the Spirit with *nous* or mind, the highest and most immaterial faculty of the human person.

Too often, however, and very early in Christian history, Paul's doctrine was misread as if he were opposing the life of our soul, something good, to the life of our flesh or body, something evil. The same misreading has also affected two sayings of Jesus reported in *The Gospel according to Matthew* (10:28 and 16:26) in which Jesus spoke of body and soul or of losing one's life. In Jesus' teaching the word for "soul" (in Greek *psyche*) would not have been that which is the spiritual principle of Greek philosophy; it is, rather, the idea and reality expressed in Hebrew by *nephesh*, that is, the *seat of supernatural life* and the *object of supernatural salvation*. To "lose one's soul," therefore, is to lose the totality of one's self as a living, conscious subject, including the body and emotions springing from sense powers. To "save one's soul" is to save the totality of one's self. That is why the resurrection of the whole being, including the body, is so important in biblical teaching.

Early Church Theologians

Already in some early theologies in the church we begin to see this misreading and deflection of thought and terminology. In order to urge people to holiness, theologians mixed the biblical message with Stoic philosophy, Platonist philosophy, and sometimes traces of Gnosticism or Manichaeism, even though they also opposed these last two doctrines. Stoics looked on the feelings, the emotions, and the body as impediments to virtuous living. The ideal was *apatheia,* a lack of feeling. Our English word *apathy* is rooted in this Greek word. Furthermore, Platonists and neo-Platonists saw the sensible world as a shadow of the really real, the true reality found in the unchanging world of ideas, which for them was the realm of the immaterial, the spiritual in the sense of that which is opposed to the material. Change, and history working itself out through change, were considered a weakness and a falling away from the realm of the unchanging and eternal, the spiritual. The "One" was the highest reality. Therefore, they had trouble with the "many," with diversity, and sought to reduce or lead all multiple, diverse things back to the "One." Both Gnostics and Manichaeans despised the material and the bodily, seeing them either as the product of sinful error among the gods or as the creation of an evil creator god. Theologians in the eastern and western branches of Christianity were influenced in varying degrees by these currents of thought. They adopted Stoicism and Platonism with great enthusiasm because these doctrines seemed to point to a lofty elevated life.

In the West, some of these ideas were filtered through thinkers like Ambrose and Augustine, great persons who have served Christianity well in so many ways but who also established certain patterns that have not been helpful. Augustine's Platonism led him to stress the world as a place of signs pointing to the truly real. For Augustine, one finds this truly real—ultimately God the Father, Son, and Holy Spirit—by going from the exterior world to the interior, going within oneself, and then moving from the lower to the higher in oneself and from there to God. The truest spiritual life is led in the interior of the mind, and Augustine constantly moves along what Anton Pegis has called the "Augustinian highway," from without to within, from oneself to God. Hence a tendency to see true life in the Spirit as interior life.

Another important influence on attitudes in spirituality was the doctrine of original sin, especially as developed in the West. According to Augustine original sin and its dire effects were passed on through the marriage act because, however good marriage is in itself, intercourse inevitably involves some disorder or sin, at least a venial sin. Pleasure in marriage had to be justified for Augustine by reason of the benefit of children, although Augustine does include among the goods of marriage the fidelity of the couple to each other as well as the symbolic quality of their marriage, that is, its symbolizing the union of Christ and the church (which was seen as the reason for the indissolubility of marriage).

Anselm in the late Eleventh Century and Thomas Aquinas in the Thirteenth Century strongly modified Augustine's close link between original sin and disordered concupiscence by stressing that the initial disorder of the human *will* to God was central. Nevertheless, Augustine's influence remained strong, so much so that Luther's basically personal problems grew out of his attempts to come to terms with Augustine's doctrine of concupiscence in relation to original sin. Earlier than Luther, in the Twelfth Century, Peter Lombard, a theologian whose *Book of Sentences* became the standard textbook for theologians in the universities of Europe, summarized the role of sacraments as follows: some sacraments, such as baptism, are both a remedy against sin and bestower of grace; other sacraments such as Eucharist and orders simply confer grace. There is one sacrament that is *only* a remedy against sin, and that is matrimony.[3] This was hardly a positive spirituality for marriage or for lay persons who lived in a secular culture or even in a religious society.

Other Historical Forces at Work

Two other historical forces affected spirituality for lay persons. In the Fourteenth Century, theology became divorced from the living sources of scripture and sound patristic tradition, losing itself instead in endless subtle disputations. This drove those seeking nourishment for life in the Spirit to separate a consideration of spirituality from theology. This led to the development of "spiritual theology" or "the theology of the spiritual life" over against the theology of the schools. Although such a development might seem a harmless and even necessary development, a continuation of the type of theology favored in the monasteries, what it did in effect was to separate spirituality from many areas of theology that are absolutely essential to a full life in the Spirit. The new spiritual theology tended to stress the areas of prayer, asceticism, mortification, practice of specific virtues, the laws of growth in holiness. This was all very good, but too often divorced from the great mysteries of faith on which true life in the Spirit must draw. Thus, the rich doctrines of the Father, Son, and Holy Spirit in trinitarian theology and in their missions and indwelling were not examined so thoroughly as they should have

---

[3] Peter Lombard, *Sententiae in IV libris distinctae*, distinctio 2, capitulum 1.

been, nor were they integrated into spiritual life. Christ, his grace and his headship as well as a sound theology of his saving work, frequently failed to be examined carefully in themselves and therefore lacked a beneficial and corrective influence on uncritically assumed tenets and practices in spirituality. For example, the practice of persons seeking holiness offering themselves to God as "victim souls" to be punished for the sins of others grew out of a false theology of Christ's saving work. Christ did not save the human family by being punished by God for is sins rather than by his loving obedience to the Father in fidelity, a fidelity and obedience to the Gospel pushed to the point of death. Again, sacraments and liturgy were neglected as important elements of life in the Spirit. In the area of grace, one could find elements of practical Pelagianism or semi-Pelagianism, that is, that the human person starts things off in the spiritual life and calls on God for help only when the going gets difficult.

A reversal, entirely in line with the fundamental orientation of Aquinas' scriptural commentaries and *Summa theologiae,* is going on today. This trend opposes the isolation of spiritual theology from the important theological themes that should help it. Theology once again is drinking deeply from Scripture and from the great saintly theologians of the past. It is more concerned with the life of the Christian in the Spirit. Some working in spirituality are insisting that any spiritual guidance must include attention to the whole theological dimension and, beyond that, attention to the sociological, psychological, and cultural elements that operate in the present and in any spiritual writer of the past who is studied and used. Spirituality is seen as embracing the life of the whole person. Social life—life in the family, at work, in recreation, in society as a whole—is viewed as integral to spiritual life. This is as much a part of the life of the Spirit in a Christian as is her or his personal devotion and the elements that go into this. The two cannot be separated; they were not so separated by Thomas Aquinas. Here he teaches important lessons.

The second historical force is basic to this topic: the growing recognition of the intrinsic value and worth of the natural created order. This recognition began in the Twelfth Century and took on new vigor in the Thirteenth Century, especially in Albert the Great and Thomas Aquinas, and has grown ever since. The result was that the realm of nature, and with it the role of the secular, began to be asserted more strongly. The autonomy of the natural, the independence of the secular in relation to the sacred and in particular to the Church became one of the major foci of western cultural history as well as an area of political and economic conflict. As this long struggle continued, and as an ever-increasing growth of marvelous achievements taking place in the created order and in secular humanism, the necessary distinction between the sacred and the secular tended to become more and more a separation and even an opposition. Hence there grew a constantly greater hostility and isolation of the church from the secular realm. Christ's faithful lay persons were caught in the midst of this conflict. They wanted to live by faith and the Spirit. Still, how were they to function in a society constantly more impatient with the church and its "interference" in human progress?

The Augustinian line that flourished in most of western Christian spirituality (except for the Thomist line) viewed nature and creation as so wounded by original sin that it is full of vanity and has worth only if it is healed by the grace that comes through Christ and his church. In this line of thought, created reality tends towards nothingness. God must be there with grace continually to keep creation from fading into the nothingness of sin. Of course, not all creation is evil, but its function as something good is to arouse our minds to think of God and stimulate our hearts to praise God. The political and social orders serve God; often this was taken to mean that they should serve the Church. Such a spirituality could provide little help for the lay person intensely involved in the secular sphere. It called such lay persons to condemn much of the very area where they had to work out their lives. This conflict of attitudes is well expressed by Gabriel Marcel.

> My most intimate and most unshakable conviction—too bad for orthodoxy if it is heretical—is that, whatever so many spiritual and learned men may have said, God in no way wants to be loved by us in opposition to the creature, but wants to be glorified through the creature and starting from the creature. That is why I cannot bear so many spiritual writings. That God, who is set up against all that is created and who is in some way jealous of his own handiwork, that is only an idol in my eyes. It is a relief for me to have written this. And I declare that until I retract this I shall be insincere whenever I seem to state anything contrary to what l have just written.[4]

Marcel wondered about the orthodoxy of his view. It is too bad that he did not know Albert the Great and Thomas Aquinas better because he would have found exactly his own viewpoint in them. To be sure, they did not neglect sin and the disorder it has introduced into human affairs and into human persons throughout history, but their major contribution was to accept nature and, so to speak, give nature its due. Although

---

[4] Marcel, *Journal metaphysique*, March 5, 1933.

they did not work out all the implications of their positions, their attitudes and doctrines prepared the way for a spirituality that is appropriate to lay people living and working in secular society. Pope Leo XIII's fostering of the study of Thomas Aquinas helped bring his views into relation with modem society, and the successive teachings of the popes and other leaders influenced by Aquinas gradually helped the Church to come to a more realistic appraisal of, and even a cooperation with the secular society that had so long been mistrusted and condemned. Thinkers in the Thomist line, such as Jacques Maritain, Étienne Gilson, M.-D. Chenu, Yves Congar, Karl Rahner, and others, furthered this more positive view of nature, secular achievements, and activity, always with the Christian working of grace – but still respecting the role of the natural order and the secular values that go with it.

For Thomas and his followers there is no self-contained natural order with its own absolute and ultimate end. The absolutely final end of all men and women consists in the beatific vision overflowing in love, and no one can be truly happy without achieving this end. Albert and Thomas and their followers agree with Augustine and all others on this (see *ST* I-II, q. 3, a. 8). For Thomas, however, there are intermediate or connatural ends to nature and to secular activity that can be identified and respected (see *ST* I-II, q. 68, a. 2[5]). These limited or intermediate finalities or ends of natures and human institutions are worthwhile in themselves and must be respected. When we do this, when we develop these intermediate finalities to the full, we give greater glory to God than if we simply use them as a tool of the Church or religion.

---

[5] References to the *Summa theologiae* (*ST*) are in the text.

Long ago Irenaeus of Lyons had said that the glory of God is the human person become fully alive.[6] Teilhard de Chardin developed similar notions in his book *The Divine Milieu*. So often, he said, our work was seen as simply something to be done with a good intention, something to be offered up in the morning prayer. It didn't matter what we did, for one's intention was the important thing. Monks wove baskets to keep themselves busy while they prayed; then they took the baskets apart and started over again. Teilhard countered: Our work done in the world is part of one's loving service of the Lord. The kind of work, its effects and its influence on society are all important for advancing human history towards its fulfilment in Christ. Therefore, one's work is integral to one's life in the Spirit - to one's spirituality. Gustave Thils, theologian of Louvain, did much work on what he called "the theology of earthly realities," while others developed a theology of work. All this fed into the Second Vatican Council and resulted in its accepting in a new positive way the advances made in the secular sphere. It encouraged Christians to work in the world for its advancement. History and society are not just hockey rinks or baseball fields where Christians can go and play games without the final outcome mattering one bit so long as they play in such a way as not to fall into sin and thereby lose their "souls." Work in human society is part of the development of human history, part of the coming of the kingdom and rule of Christ. The Risen Lord directs all history to its goal, its fulfillment:

---

[6] Irenaeus, *Adversus haereses* 4, 20, 7. "*Gloria enim Dei vivens homo.*" Irenaeus, however, added a phrase that is often forgotten: "*Vita autem hominis visio Dei.*" "We are most fully alive when we see God." He goes on to say that Christ, the Word of God, is the most perfect manifestation of the Father and gives life most fully to those who see God through this Word's manifestation.

this can be achieved without baptizing every element of human history or making it all explicitly Christian.

For Aquinas, the work that Christ's faithful do in the world is their appropriate way to give glory to God. This is accomplished not just by offering it up with a good intention, but by seeing whatever one is doing through to its perfection - not always an easy job given the tendencies within and without us. (One thinks of businessmen or politicians having to operate in a society that could be called worldly in the negative sense).

Some Particular Themes in Thomas Aquinas

The basic teaching of Thomas Aquinas is important for Christians especially today as they study theology and are active in ministry.

(a) Giving value to the uniqueness of each person's spirituality

Thomas says that "the person, that is, someone subsisting in a rational nature, is the most perfect reality in all nature" (*ST* I, q. 29, a.3.) In his view, each person is unique. Each is constituted as a person by a unique act of existing. Each has a personal existence and history, a personal development and holiness, to be achieved under God's gracious help, that is his or her own. No one else can give the particular and special glory to God that each person is called to give uniquely in and through his or her personal history. Just as the variety of creatures makes a more perfect universe and gives more glory to God, so the variety and differing intensity of God's grace in the lives of persons contributes more to the beauty and perfection of the Church (and so to God's glory) than if everyone had the same kind and degree of grace (*ST* I, q. 112, a. 4). This means that a man, a woman has a unique role to play, a unique destiny. I, living and working in a particular time and place with a particular kind of activity, give glory to God. Moreover, none of this can be separated from my life in the Spirit.

(b) An ecological principle

The theme in Aquinas that has been mentioned with respect to the individuality of persons can also serve as a basic principle for ecological concerns. He is no monist. He exults in the diversity of creatures (as well as of individuals). Glory is given to God by this diversity: each species of creatures shows forth God's wisdom and goodness in a way that others cannot (*ST* I, q. 47, a. 1; q. 44, a. 4). Aquinas' spirituality is not only a God-originating spirituality but also a God-oriented spirituality. Creation is cherished and given its due but his spirituality is not a creation or creation-centered spirituality. Preserving each individual species is for the Dominican a service of God's glory. Christians, however, should especially be interested in ecology. Aquinas' teaching links their ecological concerns with their life in the Spirit.

(c) The wholeness of the human person: passions or emotions as sharing morality

Another historical influence in the West was the penetration of the Aristotelian distinction of soul and body in terms of human psychology. The danger was that Aristotle's immaterial soul would be identified with the spiritual, while the material body would be linked with the flesh. When this happened, it re-enforced the earlier misreading of Paul and Matthew and supported unhelpful influences by philosophers. The spiritual life would be thought of as the life of the soul, and material elements are considered as outside the spiritual.

Thomas Aquinas was not simply an Aristotelian. If he used the Aristotelian soul-body distinction rather than the Platonic psychology of spirit, soul, and flesh, his own distinct and original philosophy of being (*esse*) led him far beyond Aristotle. He views the human person as an integral whole in which body and soul are united in and by the human person's one, unique act of existing (*esse* or *actus essendi*). This strongly rejected any dualism in the human person, whether that of Platonism, Stoicism, Manichaeism, or badly applied Aristotelianism.

As a result, Aquinas saw the sense appetites, as well as the passions or emotions flowing from them, as good when ordered *from within* by the virtues of moderation (temperance) and courage (fortitude). Emotions share in the moral goodness of well-ordered actions chosen by the will or in the moral evil of disordered actions chosen by the will. They are not ordered from outside by repression or by a domineering rule coming from the will but rather by a guiding interior movement of virtue, a stance that comes after training, discipline, and asceticism (see *ST* I-II, q. 24, aa. 1&3). When these virtues are possessed in a high degree of intensity (Christ is the supreme exemplar of this), passionately strong acts can flow spontaneously from them because they will be well-ordered within by the virtues. This was the case when Christ was angry, or when he loved Martha, Mary, and Lazarus to the point of shedding tears of sadness over Lazarus' death, or when he showed amazement at the centurion's faith (see *ST* III, q. 15). A modem Catholic psychiatrist, Conrad Baars, laments the fact that Aquinas' doctrine was not followed in practice. Generations of Catholics were warped by the repressive views inherited from other spiritual traditions in Catholicism.[7] This affected the attitude towards all of the spiritual life. A spiritual life was conceived more as an interior life to be led in separation from the changing, unsubstantial, and even wicked world. The ideal

---

[7] See the writings of Conrad Baars.

therefore often became the life of monasteries and convents withdrawn from the world and society.

In earlier centuries, there was a sense of vocation developed by some for lay persons: this is seen in the guilds and in the ideals of knighthood. By and large spirituality for lay people working in society - which itself was considered something to be sacralized and not left secular - was patterned as much as possible on that of monks, friars, or nuns.

The effects of this can be seen in Catholic piety and spirituality lasting up to the early part of the Twentieth Century. Priests spoke of their pastoral duty as the cure of souls, or asked how many souls there were in a parish. St Thérèse of Lisieux's excellent autobiography was entitled *L'histoire d'une âme* (*The Life of a Soul*), and translations of books by French authors often used the word "soul" instead of referring to the whole human person. Most of the spiritual treatises that appeared in the earlier decades of our century were written by and for monks and other religious. They often reflected a fear of the world as a place of danger or temptation, a place from which to retire in order to foster spiritual life.

(d) The human person as image of God and of the Trinity

When it comes to the human person's deliberation and choices in her or his human activity (the very stuff of our spirituality so long as we do not shut spirituality into some narrow area divorced from all human activity and its moral quality), Aquinas' teaching on the human person as an image of God and of the Trinity is crucial. Father Ignatius Eschmann, my Dominican professor at the Pontifical Institute of Medieval Studies, used to become so excited as he quoted and carefully analyzed the short preface Thomas Aquinas wrote at the start of the *prima secundae* of the *Summa theologiae*. That simple prelude gave the overarching view governing all that was to follow about the end of the human person, human will, the human passions, the virtues, gifts of the Holy Spirit, vices, and commands. In this prologue Thomas says: "The human person (*homo*) is made according to in God's image (a*d imaginem Dei).*" The reader notes the forceful Latin accusative case, *imaginem,* implying a dynamic tendency and activity in the created human being. "This, as John Damascene indicated, means that as image the human person is an intellectual being endowed with freedom of choice and with power to act through his or her self [i.e., as primary or responsible agent]. We have spoken about the exemplar of the human person, that is, God, as well as of all that has come forth in creation from God's power by God's willing them. Now it remains for us to examine God's image, that is to say, the human person in so far as this human person is also..." Here Aquinas writes *et*, a marvelous two-letter word pregnant with vast implications. He continues: "...And, the source of actions that are her or his own, in that the person has free choice and power to perform his or her actions. So we must first examine the final end of human life, and then the means by which the human person can either reach or fail to reach this end: for the end gives us the reasons or notions whereby we can judge how human activities are ordered to that end. And since the final end of human life is declared to be beatitude, we must first consider the ultimate end taken generally, and then beatitude."[8]

---

[8] The force of the expression, "The end gives us the reasons or notions whereby we can judge how human activities are ordered to that end" should be noted. This points to Thomas' nature-based outlook that seeks moral-spiritual judgments by looking to the nature of things and their finalities as well of the finalities of their actions. Later nominalism or conceptualism destroyed this intrinsicism and was forced to turn to the will of the lawgiver, to law, and hence to obligations as the basis of moral judgments, with the consequent development of casuistry as

Each human person is the prime agent of his or her own spiritual-moral life and decisions, always of course dependent on God, but not in the first instance dependent on commands, ordinances, obedience, direction, or counseling by others. It is for the human person—"a little god" (if we may so call the human person) imitating the infinite God—to exercise mind, free choice, and movement to action.[9]

(e) Finding the will of God

If we have a unique personhood and so a unique spirituality, how do we find God's will for us, how do we live out our unique role? Too often God's will and our way of finding it are conceived as an entirely divine scenario all pre-arranged. Woe betide us if we do not discover the elements of that fixed scenario and conform to its details. We do not, however, receive a special revelation from God. What we are to do should be seen in tandem with God's will for us *in this present moment*. God in eternity is actively present here and now to help me find the divine will. Here and now I am to try to judge what is the best, the just and loving thing to do. I am to study, gather information, try to foresee the consequences of a decision, pray over it, perhaps seek counsel -- but not by blind obedience to another. I am a responsible lay person having to make a decision in my own realm. If I eliminate any personal prejudice or unruly passion, and then make my decision, I can be sure that I am in fact doing God's will.

That is what God's will is for me: to make a free decision under the influence of God's grace, using all the

---

a prime tool in such judgments.

[9] For this and what follows see *ST* I-II, q. 14, "On counsel," a *consilium* which precedes "choice." For Thomas, this act of taking counsel is done by the person as primary agent, investigating and judging what is to be done. Only in passing does he mention the usefulness of consulting others on the way to one's own decision.

means available to me. Later on I might look back and think another decision might have been better. No matter, at the time of the decision I did all I could and so I did God's will. Aquinas will say very strongly that even if my conscience, my final decision about the goodness or evil of an act, is erroneous, it must be followed and one would be blameworthy for not following an objectively erroneous conscience.[10]

(f) A spirituality of prudence guided by the Holy Spirit

For lay persons, a spirituality of prudence under the guidance of the Holy Spirit is more appropriate than a spirituality dominated by the idea of obedience to laws that try to cover every possibility, or of obedience to a spiritual director or authority whose competence and office cannot extend to the details of life.[11] Some lay persons select spiritual *directors* and seek to obey them in all things as if they gave forth the voice of God. This is wrong. Such a person should be sought for *assistance* in *self*-counselling, for help in sorting things out on the way to making *one's own* decisions. Such an assistant should never be allowed to take over one's life and, especially, one's decisions.

This spirituality is firmly rooted in the healthy teaching of Thomas Aquinas. For him each human being is made unto the image of God because of our intellect, our free will, our power to act through and in ourselves - always, of course, under the influence of God's gracious help and the special aid of the gifts of the Holy Spirit, in

---

[10] See *ST* I-II, q. 19, aa. 3 & 4, and the remarks of T.-H. Deman in his "*renseignements techniques*" in *Saint Thomas d' Aquin: Somme théologique: La prudence* [2nd ed.] (Paris: Lethielleux, 1949) 496-506.

[11] For Thomas on prudence see *ST* II-II, qq. 47- 56. Question 52 here studies the Holy Spirit's gift of counsel. See the full commentary in Deman cited above.

particular the gifts of wisdom, understanding, knowledge, and counsel. The prudent person (and prudence can mean daring risk as well as care and caution) does look to revelation, the laws of God and the Church and of society in the secular sphere. But these cannot cover individual cases. The prudent person must make a judgment taking into account of all the particularities of each case.

A lay person working and living in secular society cannot abandon to another person in the church the individual role of being an image of God. One must examine a particular rule or command to see that it is truly good and not harmful in the circumstances that one knows better than any lawgiver, superior, or spiritual director. If we obey, we obey freely. Law and obedience cannot cover individual circumstances and situations. Therefore, the lay person needs the maturity to make a fully prudent decision within the context that only he or she knows. No priest or other person should be allowed to dictate or direct one in one's area of personal competence and decision.

(g) The New Law and the gifts of the Holy Spirit

In ordering the materials of the second part on the Christian life in his *Summa theologiae* Thomas takes a very positive view. He begins with the virtues that fasten us directly into life with God—faith, hope, and charity—and follows them with the key or cardinal virtues of prudence, justice, temperance, and fortitude. Connected with these virtues are their gifts of the Holy Spirit. The New Law, the New Covenant, is the inner presence of the Holy Spirit with gifts that lead men and women to live lives according to the Gospel—at times perhaps according to the 'foolishness' of the Gospel. Christ's faithful need this constant loving help of the Spirit to live on the high plane of faith, hope, and love directed immediately to God. All need to go beyond what reason or perhaps mundane views would prescribe and be led to the higher plane of Spirit-filled activity (see *ST* I-II, q. 68, a 2). This is true spirituality.

After these virtues infused by God with their gifts of the Holy Spirit come other virtues attached to these great virtues. Then the vices and sins opposed to the virtues are treated, habits and acts that can lead away from the God-originating and God-oriented directions a life will have as long as it does not interpose a disordered human choice in the way. Finally come the commandments, teaching guides and helps for a discipline of self that will keep the life in the Spirit from being rejected. This positive view is quite different from the approach of many of the older moralists insisting on obligations and commands as the basic way to approach morality. In fact, that dispirited moral doctrine was never seen by them or their students as a spirituality, as life in the Spirit, but as a kind of dubious foundation on which exalted social or religious states might build. There is no separation of morality and spirituality in Thomas Aquinas; moral life is life in the Spirit and life in the Spirit is moral life.

(h) Faith in God in contrast with propositions of faith and ecclesial teaching

Aquinas' teaching on faith is important here for problems faced today by people living in today's world and who wonder about this or that official teaching of the church. Faith is the assent to the very truth of God in a personal encounter in which God as First Truth "speaks," albeit in darkness, to the mind. Believers assent to that Truth under the deliberate or uncertain movement of the will itself moved by God. Faith is an encounter with the Infinite Reality of God. The statements of this faith like creeds and definitions are needed for our human way of knowing and for a community of faith united in professing its faith. But these statements or propositions are not the object or end of our faith. By faith we pass through these propositions to the very *Res*, the Infinite Mysterious Reality of God, One and Triune. A courageous gift of self like that called for by Jesus in the Gospel, relativizes to a certain extent the propositions or statements of faith. They grasp truth, but inadequately, grasp some tiny aspect of the infinite Mystery of God. There is always room for improvement, modification, change without contradiction, of these statements, and that has happened in history.[12]

The Dominican has a pregnant remark about propositions of faith, "The act of the believer does not terminate at the proposition but at the Reality [of God]" (*ST* II-II, q. 1, a. 2, ad 2). This applies forcefully to propositions included in those official teachings of the Church that are not means for plunging into the mystery of God by a gift of heart and mind. Christ's faithful need to be told and to see that not a few teachings are certainly to be respected and accepted if one has no special competence, knowledge, or experience. Still they are not matters of faith and can be subject to investigation and possible alteration. This is more true of ordinary theological opinions found in catechisms or summaries of Catholic doctrine.[13] There are at work here an important series of distinctions that Christ's followers need to know and keep in mind. This will help them face the problems they meet in the application of Church teaching to their personal lives.

---

[12] This is a summary of several important articles in *ST* II-II, qq. 1 & 2.

[13] For more on this see my *Faith, History, and Cultures: Stability and Change in Church Teachings*, The Père Marquette Lecture, 1991 (Milwaukee: The Marquette University Press, 1991), and "Changing Church Teachings," *Grail: An Ecumenical Journal* 6 (1990): 13-40.

(i) The presence of Christ to human history

Aquinas' teaching on the active presence and influence of the Risen Lord, Jesus Christ, to all of human history can be an important element of spirituality for those living and working in the world. In two questions at the end of his consideration of the mysteries of Christ's life, death, and exaltation, he speaks of Christ sharing through his humanity in the governing and judging power of the Father. This, of course, requires Christ's human knowledge and presence to be in some ways part of the course of human history.

There is an unusual teaching about how this active presence of the human Christ takes place in us. The Father, Son, and Holy Spirit, by their gift to men and women are the principal cause of that intense modification, elevation, and heightening of our being and activity that we call grace. But, he adds—and in this he breaks new ground in comparison with all his predecessors—the human Christ is in a certain way the cause of the gift of grace, for his human nature serves the divinity as an instrumental cause to confer this gift on men and women. Pursuing this idea, he makes a startling comparison between Christ's presence to confer and maintain grace and God's presence to confer and maintain our very being or existing. "Because Christ in a certain way (*quodammodo*) pours the effects of grace into all rational creatures, it follows that in a certain way (*quodammodo*) he is the principle of all grace according to his humanity, as God is the principle of all being (*esse*). Hence, as in God every perfection of being (*essendi*) is united, so in Christ is found every fullness of grace and virtue, through which [fullness] he is able not only to perform works of grace but also to lead others into grace. And in this way he has the notion of head."[14]

We should reflect on and discover the active presence and influence, usually hidden, of Jesus Christ, the Risen Lord in all of Christian life and indeed into all of human history. For Christ is Lord of the whole of human history and of the cosmos and its development. He intervenes not to destroy the good developments of the created order but to further its advancement until his final coming when his rule will be visible and will be explicitly recognized by all.

By this presence Jesus Christ is a source of hope for persons working in society. Its natural finalities must be fostered and not simply twisted to serve the sacred. It is still under Christ's rule and presence, and this should be a constant source of real hope for all. Christ is not reserved just to churches or to a narrow spirituality. If we can find him in churches, liturgy, and personal prayer, we can and must also find him present to all humanity, to all human striving in history.

Thomas Aquinas was a person of his times, and he needs completion and correction in various areas. These pages, however, have shown that many basic insights and teachings from his thinking can be valuable for the spirituality of Christ's faithful living in the world.

---

[14] Aquinas, *De Questiones Disputata, De Veritate* q. 29, a. 2. The qualifications (*quodammodo*) are introduced by Thomas in this comparison to mark the difference between God's causality and conservation of being (*esse, actus essendi*), in which there can be no instrumental cause, and the causality of the gifts of grace, in which Christ's humanity can play a part as instrumental cause. By what I like to call such a "mental genuflection" before the mystery when he is applying analogical terms to God, Thomas is alerting his readers to the limitations of the comparison even while stating an important point about Christ's causality and necessary presence in the order of grace.

SERMONS

Veritas Liberabit Vos. "The Truth Will Make You Free"
Marie-Dominique Chenu, O.P.

What kind of teacher was Thomas Aquinas? How can we be his disciples? How should we pursue the work of Thomas whose spirit is present in the specific and necessary aspects of being a conqueror? He is a conqueror through a flexible but sure mastery of theological knowledge, of a theology living within the humanities as they are evaluated and known through pressing new ideas and a perduring capability of progress. All this showed itself forcefully in the course of a terrible crisis of Christianity: it took place during the Thirteenth Century and involved the providential mission of the Friars Preachers.

A spiritual liberty like the daring and clear spiritual freedom of St. Albert and of St. Thomas is a kind of "natural law" of the Dominican Order. Particularly in serious times it stimulates, along with regular teaching and the tranquil possession of the truth, an acute but serene perspective. This serves the discernment of ideas, and a new fecundity of traditional principles now more profoundly penetrated. If this is a trait of the intellectual and spiritual physiognomy of Thomas Aquinas and a virtue of the Dominican Order attracting the confidence and sympathy of generations, it is well to sense in his writings this natural law of the Order that appears in the audacious clarity and a spiritual independence of St. Thomas Aquinas. It furthers a realistic cult of Truth, loved for itself and permeating all.

"*Veritas liberabit vos.*" The truth will set you free

I would like to mention something of the sources, the guarantees, and the conditions of spiritual liberty for all of us in our witness and fidelity to Thomas Aquinas.

The Spiritual Liberty of Thomas Aquinas

What image do we have of Thomas Aquinas? How do we see him? How do we picture him and the circumstance of his life? What kind of spiritual life did he have?

You know the magnificent portrait begun at Pisa by Franceso Traini and worked on by others like Benozzo Gozzoli, and which eventually is to be found in Santa Maria Novella in Florence: *The Triumph of Thomas Aquinas*. He sits on a throne, and near his head is the Holy Spirit. He is surrounded by the doctors of the Latin and Greek Churches, and a little below them are Aristotle and Plato. Other figures of wisdom from heaven and Earth are present. At his feet, there is a man in a humble position and wearing a turban; we know that is this is Averroes the Arab. For a long time, this has been the central picture whose theme is Thomas Aquinas and it became the source of the ordinary way of picturing him. Certainly, we find there joy, pride, and security; his triumph is ratified and guaranteed by the Church, a peaceful encouragement for our work. I am not setting this aside. But this approach recalls and supports an idea and framework that people fashioned for Aquinas once he was dead: a "school" was set up, a school focused on his writings and his relics. That installs Thomist truth in triumph on a throne; his teaching becomes official and is transformed into something highly "orthodox." When we ponder Aquinas' life and world, this approach is erroneous from the viewpoints of history, psychology, and theological education. It is fine to present all these disciples at a particular moment of triumph. This, however, neglects two painful episodes: the condemnation of 1270, and a further one after his death in 1277, condemnations that may be camouflaging revenge from some of his disciples.

Thomas Aquinas wasn't present at any triumph. Actually, a basic, spiritual attitude of his and of the psychological and historical atmosphere of his writings is conflict. The atmosphere of their creation was not one of the laurels of triumph but a spirit of conquering curiosity. This curiosity seeks out every truth, pursuing fearlessly their sources, in Aristotle and the Arabs (he has some critical words for their writings but he uses them copiously).

The case of Thomas is a typical case—but not a unique one—of Aristotle entering Christianity. For ten centuries Aristotle had been banned from Christian thinking; in thirty years of Thomas' century he was condemned three times. But then there were emerging daring public movements to "make him intelligible to the Latins" (as Albert wrote). A strong perseverance was needed just to read Aristotle. If only we could overhear Albert and Thomas discussing Aristotle between themselves, discussing perhaps how to teach him? We should not forget that Aristotle in their time was a most serious danger for Christianity. The idea of Christianity was widely spread, impregnated with religious symbolism; then there appeared a rational, independent, scientific explanation of the world. Understandably that brought a kind of anxiety – an anxiety we feel today when we experience the intellectual life of modern thinkers, non-Christians, presenting their ideas and making responses to them difficult. Only an audacious freedom could accept Aristotle; this was an admirable liberty. There had to be a mastery of Aristotle and yet that awareness could not be a collapse before an Aristotelian conquest. We don't find it easy to picture how Thomas struggled with Aristotle.

Let us imagine another adversary, one who had lived in the previous century: Averroes. It took a lot of courage to enter into a dialogue with such a thinker, for he could be a threat to the entire framework of Western Christian thought. This is one of the greatest crises of Christianity. For Aquinas, the choice is not about this or that thinker, Plato or Aristotle, but over a stance, an acceptance of the entirety of Greek thought. One needs to let it enter the Christian culture, let it make the world's realities intelligible with their reasons for existence, their structures, their laws. Things have a reality, a density when you look at them with this understanding of this world. Is this not paganism, a complete misconception of Christ as king of Christians?

It is in a realization and fulfillment of this intellectual approach—and not only in the perspective—that we find the spirit of Aquinas. What is at play here is not only a theory but an "imago mundi", an image of the world, a total conception of the human being and of the religious and moral order. This requires often spiritual generosity, daring, and a balanced spiritual freedom. Thomas remains intrepid and calm, a master of his own insights, capable of penetrating the complexity of things. He sees an intellectual unity touching diverse values. He works with a breadth and depth among silent texts and noisy struggles. He is a solitary thinker even as he shares in the thinking of his generation. This is the concrete role of Thomas Aquinas: it is not a question of beginning a school but of shaping of a civilization.

Aquinas' Contact with his Contemporaries

The situation of Thomas Aquinas is the situation of the Friars Preachers in Christianity at that time. In those years there is an extensive social upheaval: feudalism seems consumed by its own privileges, and there is the rise of a threatening class. Politically this is the "communes" and socially it is the "corporations."

In the world of the spirit parallel to social change there is a discovery of antiquity in literary and philosophical works. For the young in a civilization arriving at maturity there is a frenetic curiosity along with political intemperance within the social and economic upheavals. Aristotle will enter, although this will be in original ways. The religious institutions are solidly committed to their routines. So there is, at times, a rupture, even a radical innovation in the religious institutions as they seek to recapture the attention of their contemporaries.

It is startling to recall that Thomas Aquinas was very much a feudal person. But he refused the abbacy of Monte Casino and broke with every regime to gain spiritual liberty, to enjoy the institutional liberty of the Dominican Order so that he could fashion his theological liberty. He was friends with the professors in the Faculty of Arts as they sought to learn a great deal more from antique culture. There were protests against the Aristotelianism of Aquinas; there was the scandal of the pious and the devotionally oriented towards was what new, a conflict that existed also within the Dominicans.

We should recall that Thomas Aquinas lived in the age of Louis IX and Fredrick II, at the time when communes attained their freedom and a time when change transformed the economy as corporations bore witness to the maturity of the middle class. In the same years, Notre Dame of Paris was built, the Roman de la Rose was written, and the images and symbolic signs decorating the facades of the cathedrals were executed. And too, Christianity had not lost hope of conquering or converting Islam.

Thomas Aquinas was a teacher: a daring one and a balanced one. His intellectual strategy created a civilization. He seemed to have an independence, a freedom both external and internal. His clarity and his spiritual liberty are traits of someone who is creating and changing public intellectual life. He has a sharp and focused methodology for knowing and yet enjoys a high personal contemplation of truth. Truth fueled his fervor for public life as it guaranteed his scientific methodology for fields of knowledge.

These sources, conditions, and guarantees assist us in having a spiritual freedom in the Twentieth Century as Thomas Aquinas did in the thirteenth.

Our Spiritual Freedom

Every theological structure—and we include here that fashioned by Thomas Aquinas—has a certain relativism. The fullness of faith exceeds theological constructs. A commitment to faith and a commitment to theology – each has a different intensity. Theology is founded on liberty and daring. Theology is daring precisely because a deeper knowledge and a free, primal contemplation of faith is something more. As theologians, we are daring in our contacts with our contemporaries, and we remain quite free to draw for our own use that which in the original creations of philosophers and historians is useful for our theological work.

At the heart of theology is not good will or friendly liberalism but a perception living from the very laws of theological knowledge: the "given" of faith enters into a "construction" of reason. In this way we are progressive, conquerors, free according to the example of our teacher, Aquinas.

Aquinas with his followers have found themselves in a situation of crisis more than once. I have often compared the state of Christianity in the Thirteenth Century and the state of Christianity in the Sixteenth

Century. This is not arbitrary or rhetorical, a verbal exercise. Actually, there is an analogous crisis in the two periods. In both there is the birth of a new world. Christianity is influenced by economic crises, social crises, doctrinal crises – by a crisis in the very expansion of Christianity. In the Sixteenth Century you had the expansion of the world, not only geographical but cultural, economic and social. Theologians had also been surprised at the times of the Renaissance and the Reformation. There were new kinds of natural science that they sought to draw into their thought. They did that but not without a struggle, for they could not see the future.

Certainly, in the course of history things were lost: there were defeats. For the past three centuries Christianity has been marginalized, existing in a kind of exile from the contemporary ways in which people think. Sometimes it seems that Aquinas in those years has been for us a cumbersome inheritance, and that we work only to be assured we have not lost what was simply retained. Some have built ramparts around a fortress – and it might be an impressive fortress. Nonetheless, too often we have been responding to the same problems, problems that are no longer relevant, and we have worked to avoid understanding today's problems. A tragic paradox. In place of being free people, a particular truth has made us prisoners. The truth – only birth can bring life. Each day in us there must be something of giving birth, and then growth, piece by piece, word by word, day by day.

This is risky, certainly, but it is the risk of being alive. It is better to live with some risk than to retreat from emptiness and decay, thinking wrongly that one has the truth, for the truth is always fresh and new.

The truth is not a closed world in which one installs oneself, comfortably resting. If we reach the point where we only want to stay inside our walls because our enemies are outside—enemies who in various paths following apparently erroneous directions and have conquered what is outside of our fortress—there will be no need to have a fortress, or sustain a defense. All that might be defended will be dead.

Aristotle is always besieging the walls of Christianity. He is always seductive and rather dangerous because he has his own treasures. Even more because he proposes a teaching that would nourish human beings. Let us seek to find, still, within ourselves the intellectual magnanimity of Thomas Aquinas. We want to be totally given to truth. Let's not be afraid of the risks that come with spiritual freedom. "The Truth will set you free."

Thomas Aquinas, Servant of the Word
Edward Schillebeeckx, O.P.

Rarely has human thinking resembled liturgy as much as it did with Thomas Aquinas. This appears clearly from two revealing events in his life, and from his unequivocal declaration of his own project.

First, on a Holy Thursday, while his confreres were carrying out the liturgies of Holy Week in choir, Thomas was editing a small work *Declaratio quaestionum ad Magistrum Ordinis*. On a second occasion, while he was spending time outside his priory (occupied with the financial affairs of his family), he wrote his work *De Substantiis Separatis*. He commented on its composition in this way. "I have to make up through study and writing the time that I cannot devote to the singing of the psalms." These two events are rightly understood and are significant when we see them in light of Thomas' program for his life.

Writing—as he rarely did—in the first person singular, Aquinas formulated boldly in his first great work, the *Summa contra Gentiles* how he saw the mission of his own life. "I see clearly that the primary task of my life is to let God speak through all my words, thoughts, and feelings." Thomas sees his general vocation to be one of serving God by speaking of him to other people. The reason for his life lies in a particular service of love for others, in serving his fellow human beings through his being involved with God and sharing those experiences and reflections about God with others. Thinking is a religious activity involving God and other beings; it is a service to humanity. This service for Thomas was a liturgy. Thinking itself becomes here both liturgy and apostolate; thinking is the material he makes holy and offers to God. At the same time, through this material and activity he is of service to his fellow human beings.

As a theologian, Thomas Aquinas is a servant of God and of human beings. He experienced the reality of the word "servant" in a feudal context where the poor attended their lord on whom they were dependent in all things. They felt themselves to be a commodity, a possession moving from one person to another in full alienation from themselves and in an absolute appropriation by a feudal lord. Thomas called his lordly service and subservience "the ministry of truth" (*ministerium veritatis*). His inaugural address on the occasion of his promotion to *bacchalaureus biblicus*, a beginning teacher of the Scriptures, is concerned very much with "serving the truth." He sees himself as "a doctor of truth" (*doctor veritatis*).

I like to consider the life of Thomas Aquinas as a priestly doctorate: it is a priestly service to the word in a format that is thoroughly thought out and appropriate to its time.

As a theologian, Aquinas abides in the faith through the entire power of his human reflection. He is aware that theology is a scientific study of a subject that is not scientific: this subject matter is not under the control of scientific verification, and is a subject offered to those who believe. They can, however, reflect on this subject to the extent that in thinking they can rise above thought to a child-like acceptance of God's self-evidence, something that for us, problematic people, is, of course a mystery and may at times also become a problem. It is remarkable that this consummate theologian admits that he daily prays to God that he not lose the faith. He says this explicitly in one of the prayers that we have written in his own hand.

Not to lose the faith! Aquinas sees in this a double meaning. It means, first, that his theological thinking ought never to diminish or dilute the word of God's revelation. Secondly, it means that he ought never to present as God's sovereign word what is in fact human and transitory teaching. This would be to burden others with a yoke that is not of God but has been fashioned by theologians.

First, the theologian ought never diminish or dilute the faith. The service of the truth, this liturgy of a divine work (*opus divinum*), implies that he accept the Other, God, as other, so that the reality he reflects upon as a theologian is not distorted by how creative imagining. Rather, he should mold his thinking according to the self-revealed image of God. As a servant of the truth, Thomas is attached to the Other, God, precisely as he has manifested himself to us. Thomas has no patience with a kind of blindness that causes people to be selective in terms of the divine truth. To gloss over a single facet of that truth would mean being unfaithful to his priestly doctorate.

Secondly, the theologian ought never to present as God's word something that is not God's word. For Thomas, faithfulness to God's word is also a form of not losing the faith. Here he has an unusual sensitivity that found expression in the phrases *derisus infidelium* and *articulus fidei*. I have encountered the former expression at least twenty times in his writings; he means by it that we should not present the faith in such a way that it appears naïve, passé, and ludicrous to the non-believer. In modern terms, this indicates the need for a continual reinterpretation of dogma in line with the dogma itself, and so a certain measure of demythologizing is required by loyalty to the truth. Thomas is also careful to ascertain whether or not he is dealing with an *articulus fidei*, an article of faith, that is, a religious truth that can be known only through revelation and cannot be arrived at by human thought alone. This direction is shown in his concern for not offending the thought of others, for allowing human thought freedom in its own domain, and for making a clear distinction between God's revealing word and human speculations.

Aquinas' perceptive concern with not obscuring or reducing the faith explains also the fact that he battles, equally, on two fronts to present this faith, to accept God as the Other.

On one front, he fights against various forms of fundamentalistic integralism that would make a farce out of genuine confrontation. His library is full of works considered suspect by some of the theologians and bishops of his day, for instance, the latest novelties of pagan philosophers of Jewish-Arabic thinkers. This amount to a kind of "medieval modernism" in reference to which Thomas' confrere Albert the Great—no less holy but more excitable—wrote: "Our opponents are too lazy to study these writings. They merely leaf through them in order to charge us with whatever heresies and errors they may run across. Thereby they feel that they are doing Christendom a service. They are the ones who have murdered Socrates, who drove Plato away, and whose machinations have banned Aristotle from the universities." Thomas thought the same but said nothing. He kept working and constructed a new Christian synthesis from these "modern writings."

A second front on which Aquinas struggled for the authenticity of the faith was the academic conflicts where he was an opponent of all kinds of excessive progressivism like the excesses of Siger of Brabant and his associates. Those university teachers brought discredit to Thomas' progressive thinking. Because they cast suspicion on his life work of service to the truth, they made the usually serene and imperturbable Aquinas quite angry. This context of a progressive perspective that was excessive and thereby threatened authentic renewal furthered its opposite: a reactionary fundamentalism. Here we find Thomas, remarkably, using uncommon epithets like *stupidum*, *absurdum*, and *stupidissimum*.

When we look for the key to the life of this man of study we find it in his own words. At the time of his last reception of the Eucharist, just before his death, he said: "Jesus – for the love of whom I have studied, have stayed awake nights, have preached and taught. *'Jesus...pro cuius amore!'*" Here we have no ivory tower scholarship, no ambition; intellectual curiosity does not describe Aquinas' life of study but his generous love for a living person, Jesus Christ. On his way to the Council of Lyon where he was to be a *peritus* at the Council and created a cardinal (along with his colleague, Bonaventure), Thomas asked God that he might rather die than be a Cardinal in Rome. Bonaventure did become a Cardinal, but Thomas died on the way to Lyon. If being a Cardinal meant the end of his "priestly doctorate" it was better for him to die. His task was accomplished.

For us, however, his unfinished *Summa* is a constant reminder that the work of the priestly doctorate is always an unfinished life work. Every generation must begin it anew and press forward.

"*Jesus, pro cujus amore*" – because Thomas Aquinas loved. Love is the form of the priestly, ministerial doctorate. That is why he is a saint, and an unusual saint. That is why we celebrate with gratitude his life as a shining example for all theologians.

EXPORING THOMAS AQUINAS

Thomas Aquinas: Friar, Theologian, and Mystic

Karl Rahner, S.J.

To reflect upon Thomas Aquinas as a patron of theological education does not mean simply to think back on someone prominent in history or to sketch an intellectual influence on Western thought. We are Christians and thereby we are linked to him. He is a fellow Christian now in the communion of saints. Christians who have gone before us into the assembly of saints are not dead. They are alive. They live in a realm of fulfillment: that is, they live in the true Reality powerful and present among us today. Some of them we call by name. So these Christian women and men can be more real and more important to us than theoretical principles or abstract ideas. In many ways, they are more real than we are, for they are with God. And too, they love us, and we love them. They are present at the eternal liturgy of heaven and intercede for us, their brothers and sisters.

The essence of their life—they are eternally saved— is given from the primal Source of all reality. They live always from a history than came and comes after them, and yet they do not belong to the depths of the past but are of the past only in the sense that they have gone ahead of us into the future, the future that is still coming to us. "The Lord with his saints" is a reality more real than we are.

In comparison to the saints' present existence, their relationship to temporality, their past history on Earth, is comparatively of little significance. The eternal and the heavenly in their present reality -- we on Earth grasp slightly, if at all, only by looking backwards at their past; their life is transformed and has entered into an eternal validation from God. To look at a saint, then, is not to look at something abstract but rather to see a real concrete person, a unique individual who is now eternally existing and affirmed, someone loving and praising, a person redeemed and blessed.

Three things strike me about one of history's Christians, Thomas Aquinas. He was a friar, a monk; he was a theologian, he was a mystic.

Thomas the Monk

To say that St. Thomas was a friar, a monk, means that he was someone who was detached from possessions, someone who gave up some things for others. Detachment can be a hard, even scandalous word. We can express its meaning in another way. Thomas Aquinas was someone who set aside what was small in order to find something bigger. He let the world run its course in order that he might touch God. Yet, this still does not do away with the scandal—Christianity is essentially this scandal—that in this earthly life we cannot have everything. A person must decide. That decision cuts through existence itself. In this life, we have to let some things go in order to find the important things. We have to die in order to live. We have to be poor in order to have possessions. We can truly believe in the godly One only if we are prepared to set aside the many.

Because Thomas as a saint knew this truth and wanted to realize it in his life he became a Friar Preacher. He became a monk, an ordinary person, poor and celibate, someone unimportant, an individual dropped into a community in which he could easily be lost. Aquinas did not need to do this in terms of his familial condition. Entering a monastery did not bring any upward modification of his social status. Further, he had no resentment about not being a success in life; he was not someone who stood out for being inaccessible. He was a strong but sensitive man: he surely had some of the family traits of his aggressive, brawling brothers who were eager to add him to their circle. He was not a religious fanatic, lacking much understanding of or interest in the captivating attractions of this world. This terrestrial world he esteemed. He gave it considerable importance in contrast to some theologies that preceded him. Nonetheless, he became a friar. He wanted God, and he saw himself called to this way of life. He had that combination of faith and realism which is unique to the Christian, and he also knew that this world's order is the disorder of sin. In the sign of the cross he saw that the present could not give what eternity promised: a total reception of the interplay of God and world, of heaven and earth; the happiness of a person and the happiness of God at the same time.

When he reached the moment of decision he moved away from the side of the world. Without any contempt for what he left behind he went in a different direction, knowing that some day he would find it all again. He entered the Dominicans realistically, soberly, and honestly without any fanaticism and without an unrealistic idealism. Thomas did not enter the Order because he was an unbalanced person, someone not quite normal who feeds on disappointments, tragedies, and failures in the world. He knew that every Christian's journey through the world meets the point where the cross is standing. Because he wanted to be a Christian, he took for his vocation (without imposing it on others and without looking down on other Christians) becoming a friar.

Thomas the Theologian

Thomas Aquinas was a member of a religious order for which the priesthood was not merely something added on. The religious life of the Dominicans was geared to the priesthood. Thereby he was in a very real sense a "secular priest," a priest for the world. And, therefore, he wanted to be a theologian. He knew that because he was sent to announce the good news of the gospel he must be a theologian. He knew that one can really preach only through the witness of life. To preach is to draw from the midst of a spiritual existence: "*contemplata aliis tradere*," "to give to others the things that you have contemplated." One's own contemplation communicated through preaching and teaching draws on the normal contribution of theology: theological study is the indispensable presupostion for this. So, Thomas became a theologian. He was a theologian for whom reality, the heart of the matter, was what counted and not quick emotional satisfaction. Sometimes he did not attend the office in choir for the sake of study.

Thomas studied and taught in the cool and clear objectivity that is the sign of a great man, the sign of someone who loves reality more than he loves his own subjective, selective curiosity. He had the courage to strive for clarity wherever clarity is possible, and he had the courage to bow before mystery where mystery remains. He could distinguish between the two in order to bring them closer to each other. He had the courage to contradict opinions that were widespread or even dominant in his time. While he never sought the sensational or made novelty a criterion of truth, he had the courage to act when he knew he was right. If he had no better solution, he would remain with the traditional point of view, although he often was aware that this view was insufficient.

In his theology Thomas Aquinas spoke about God, not about himself. He wrote theology in prose although he could write poetry. He was someone who loved to reflect, to speculate. He once remarked that he would have given Paris for John Chrysostom's commentary on the *Gospel according to Matthew*. Aquinas as a mature professor could still learn from others and revise his views. He always thought from the viewpoint of the whole, and yet had an understanding and appreciation for precise questions. He expressed his own opinion without being argumentative and without looking upon his opponents as stupid. In his voluminous works, rarely do we find a sharp word. His theological perspective is broad not because he was the sole all-encompassing theologian (such is not possible) nor because he considered himself an important professor, but because he thought "in the center of the Church" (*in medio Ecclesiae*), and because he remained open for everything which both the past and his own age could bring him.

Thomas the Mystic

When we speak of Thomas Aquinas a mystic we do not mean that he had frequent ecstasies or visions; or that he was, in the style of the Spanish mystics, introverted and concerned with his experiences. There seems to be nothing of this in his writings. And yet Thomas was a mystic: he knew about the "*Latens Deitas*," "the hidden Godhead" ("*Adoro te devote, latens Deitas*"). He knew the hidden God who directs all in silence.

He spoke of a God beyond everything, beyond whatever the holiest theology could say about the God whom he loved as inconceivable. He knew about these things not only from theory but from the experience of his heart. This experience eventually substituted silence for theological words. At the end of his life he put aside his pens and writing materials and told Friar Reginald that what he had written was "straw." At the end, he left behind the house of his life in which the light of theology burned and walked into the limitless breadth of God "as if it were night." Still, as he was dying, he did speak a little – about the *Canticle of Canticles*, that great song of love. And then he was silent. He became silent because he wanted to let God alone be heard in place of the human words Aquinas had spoken to us. He wrote that human words are shadows and similes. How right and appropriate that this silence came at the end. It had to be. It came at the end and not before, but it was from the beginning a hidden seed in whose hull much can mature. In a monastic detachment from life and in a struggle of theology concerning the light of God when the struggle for that light is paid for by the crucifying and blessed experience of the night of God, a night that is the only sunrise of an eternal light.

Thomas lives. He may seem far away. That's not so. The community of saints is close, and the appearance of being far away is only an appearance. The saints come to us overshadowed by the brilliance of the eternal God into whom they have plummeted; they recall their past centuries that have disappeared into the distance. Time matures into eternity, and God is not a god of the dead but of the living. All that has gone home to God lives. And so, Aquinas lives. The question for us is: Does our faith live? Through our faith Thomas Aquinas, among the thousand times thousand saints, can become part of our own life.

Selected Writings on Thomas Aquinas' Theology

Chenu, Marie-Dominique, *Toward Understanding St. Thomas* (Chicago: Henry Regnery, 1964).

Chenu, Marie-Dominique, *Thomas Aquinas and the Role of Theology* (Collegeville: Liturgical Press, 2002).

Farrell, Walter, *A Companion to the Summa* (New York: Sheed & Ward, 1940-1959).

Grabmann, Martin, *Thomas Aquinas, His Personality and His Thought* (New York: Longmans, Green, 1928).

O'Meara, Thomas F., *Thomas Aquinas Theologian* (Notre Dame: University of Notre Dame Press, 1997).

Principe, Walter, *Thomas Aquinas' Spirituality* (Toronto: Pontifical Institute of Medieval Studies, 1984).

Pesch, Otto, *Thomas von Aquin. Grenze und Grösse einer mittelalterlichen Theologie. Eine Einführung* (Mainz: Matthias-Grünewald, 1988).

Torrell, Jean-Pierre, *St. Thomas Aquinas*, 2 vols. (Washington, D. C., The Catholic University of America Press, 1999, 2003).

Torrell, Jean-Pierre, *Aquinas's* Summa. *Background, Structure, & Reception* (Washington, D. C., The Catholic University of America Press, 2005).

Weisheipl, James Athanasius, *Friar Thomas d'Aquino: His Life, Thought, and Work* (Washington, DC: The Catholic University of America Press, 1974).

Thomas Franklin O'Meara, O.P., is a priest of the Dominican Order. He did his doctoral studies at the University of Munich. He taught from 1966 to 1979 at Aquinas Institute (Dubuque, Iowa; now at St. Louis, Missouri), and at the University of Notre Dame from 1981 to 2004. A past president of the Catholic Theological Society of America, he has been a visiting professor at Wartburg Lutheran Seminary (Dubuque); St. Joseph's Theological Institute (Cedara, South Africa); Boston College; and St. Michael's College, University of Toronto (Canada). Among his books are: *Theology of Ministry*; *Thomas Aquinas, Theologian*; and *Vast Universe. Extraterrestrials and Christian Revelation.*

www.ingramcontent.com/pod-product-compliance
Lightning Source LLC
Chambersburg PA
CBHW060803050426
42449CB00008B/1514